◄SPEARHEA

BRANDENBURGERS

The ... ces

Please return/renew this item
by the last date shown.

SOMERSET
County Council
Libraries, Arts
& Information

SPEARHEAD

BRANDENBURGERS
The Third Reich's Special Forces

Ian Westwell

Ian Allan
PUBLISHING

Acknowledgements
Design: Tony Stocks
Maps and artwork on pages 78–9: Mark Franklin
Artwork on pages 70–1, 74–5: Jan Suermondt

Thanks to George Forty, Chris Ellis, Teddy Nevill of TRH Pictures and John Gresham for providing other illustrative material.

First published 2003

ISBN 0 7110 2979 2

Published by Ian Allan Publishing

an imprint of Ian Allan Publishing Ltd, Hersham, Surrey KT12 4RG
Printed by Ian Allan Printing Ltd, Hersham, Surrey KT12 4RG

Code 0311/A2

British Library Cataloguing in Publication Data
A CIP catalogue record for this book is available from the British Library

Note: Website information provided in the Reference section was correct when provided by the author. The publisher can accept no responsibility for this information becoming incorrect.

CONTENTS

ORIGINS & HISTORY

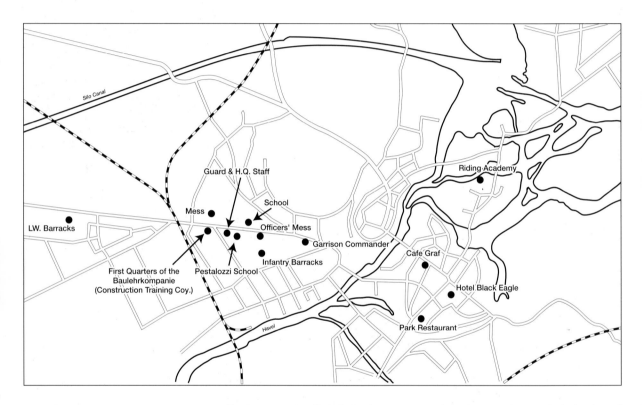

Above: Brandenburg an der Havel and the Brandenburgers' barracks.

For the most part, Nazi Germany went to war in 1939 expecting to win its battle and campaigns through the use of large conventional forces employing Blitzkrieg tactics. Little thought had been given to, or interest shown in, developing small units capable of conducting what are now commonly referred to as special operations. Although the major branches of the armed forces virtually ignored such units — and, indeed, doubted their worth, the *Abwehr* (German intelligence service) was more responsive to such ideas and successfully raised just such a formation on the eve of war. Members of this multinational clandestine force were commonly known as the 'Brandenburgers' after their chief base at Brandenburg-an-der-Havel in western Berlin, and performed roles similar to those conducted by Britain's Special Air Service or Commandos. They scored several noteworthy coups in the early campaigns of World War II, yet the ultimate fate of the Brandenburgers did not revolve around events on the battlefield but lay with the much murkier world of the internal power-politics of the Third Reich.

The *Abwehr* was formally established as a section of the Ministry of War on 21 January 1921, just over three years after the Armistice that had ended World War I and little more than two since the Treaty of Versailles, which among its provisions had outlawed the creation of a German military intelligence organisation and emasculated the country's regular armed forces. Post-1918 Europe was unstable and impoverished; Germany itself was riven by political unrest and menaced by newly independent and expansionist Poland on its eastern border. The Poles had launched several attempts to annex parts of the German provinces of Prussia, Silesia and Saxony but had been thwarted thanks only to the intervention of Freikorps units — bands of right-wing former World War I servicemen. The head of the new *Abwehr*, naval Captain Konrad Patzig, was constrained by an acute lack of funds for much of the interwar period and the meagre resources that were available were split between just two departments — Eastern and Western. *Abwehr* personnel from these departments, particularly the former, were attached to the seven military districts into which postwar Germany was divided and their main objective was to assess the military capabilities and intentions of neighbouring countries.

The activities of the *Abwehr* remained modest throughout the late 1920s and early 1930s as Germany was crippled by economic hardship and political upheaval, but its fortunes were transformed by Adolf Hitler's assumption of power on 30 January 1933. Under a new commander, 47-year-old Captain Wilhelm Canaris, from 1 January 1935, the *Abwehr*, which had developed plans for expansion during the lean years of the interwar period, received much greater funding and was transformed in size between 1936 and 1938. On top of this, its areas of responsibility expanded well beyond the original defensive remit. In February 1938 the Ministry of War was subsumed within the *Oberkommando der Wehrmacht* (OKW/High Command of the Armed Forces), the supreme planning body of the military, and a year later Canaris was made head of a transformed organisation known as the *Amt Ausland/Abwehr* (Foreign Intelligence Office), which was seen as a key department within the OKW. *Abwehr* liaison officers were also attached to the armed forces at virtually every level. In the case of the army this stretched from the *Oberkommando des Heeres* (OKH/ High Command of the Army) all the way down to divisional level in the field, and a similar pattern was followed in the air force and navy. Canaris, who had a background in clandestine operations during World War I, was well-travelled and spoke several languages, had successfully overhauled the somewhat moribund service from his offices on the Tirpitzufer in Berlin and, having gained Hitler's confidence, was rewarded with a series of rapid promotions, reaching the rank of admiral in 1940.

The much-expanded *Abwehr* consisted of several sections, whose efforts were co-ordinated and administered by *Abteilung* (Department) Z under Maj-Gen Hans Oster, Canaris's deputy and an officer later revealed to be deeply involved in the anti-Nazi resistance movement. *Amtsgruppe Ausland* was established to oversee overt intelligence gathering by military attaches and diplomats overseas, but three other *Abteilungen* conducted more clandestine operations that went far beyond the remit of the *Abwehr* in the 1920s and early 1930s. Department I was responsible for foreign espionage, the classic world of spies and spying, and Department III was given a counter-espionage role, combating foreign subversion and spying networks in both Germany and, during World War II, German-occupied lands. Unlike other intelligence services of the time, however, the *Abwehr* was not involved in one highly fruitful area of intelligence gathering — that of intercepting and decoding the enemy's radio transmissions. These operations were generally left to separate bodies within the air force, army and navy.

Partly because of this rather awkward division of responsibilities regarding radio interception, both *Abteilungen* I and III performed with mixed results immediately before and during World War II. *Abteilung* I was, perhaps, the least successful, not least because it had little experience of, or indeed time to develop, foreign spy networks before 1939.

BRANDENBURGER LOCATIONS

Initially based at Brandenburg/Havel's Generalfeldzeugmeister-Kaserne, the unit expanded to battalion size with companies based at Brandenburg; Innermanzing, Wienerwald; and Münstereifel. Later there were several smaller barracks scattered over Germany and Austria, including Rathenow/Havel (airborne), Admont/Steiermark in Austria (mountain) and Swinemünde on the Baltic Sea (coastal raiders), later at Langenargen (Lake Constance). Subunits were headquartered at various times at Baden-Unterwaltersdorf (near Vienna), Freiburg im Breisgau (Black Forest), Allenstein (East Prussia), Ploesti (Romania) and Gatron (Libya).

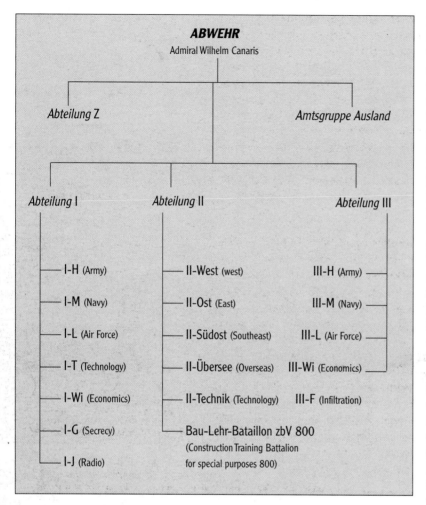

ABWEHR
Admiral Wilhelm Canaris

- **Abteilung Z**
- **Amtsgruppe Ausland**

- **Abteilung I**
  - I-H (Army)
  - I-M (Navy)
  - I-L (Air Force)
  - I-T (Technology)
  - I-Wi (Economics)
  - I-G (Secrecy)
  - I-J (Radio)

- **Abteilung II**
  - II-West (west)
  - II-Ost (East)
  - II-Südost (Southeast)
  - II-Übersee (Overseas)
  - II-Technik (Technology)
  - Bau-Lehr-Bataillon zbV 800
    (Construction Training Battalion
    for special purposes 800)

- **Abteilung III**
  - III-H (Army)
  - III-M (Navy)
  - III-L (Air Force)
  - III-Wi (Economics)
  - III-F (Infiltration)

Above: The organisation of the *Abwehr*.

Above right: Lawrence of Arabia's guerrilla tactics provided the inspiration for Theodore-Gottlieb von Hippel. Here Lawrence is seen in Arab dress in Palestine. *IWM Q59314*

Right: Hippel fought with Paul von Lettow-Vorbeck (second from right in this 1913 photograph) in East Africa in World War I. Col Paul Emil von Lettow-Vorbeck (1870–1964) was not defeated in the campaign, although he surrendered in the end to British troops. Returning to Germany a national hero and highly regarded by his enemies, Lettow-Vorbeck joined the Freikorps, and successfully crushed Spartacist forces in Hamburg. But he opposed the Nazis, fell on bad times and when, after World War II Jan Smuts, his former opponent, heard that he was living in destitution, Smuts arranged for him to receive a small pension which he received until his death on 9 March 1964 at the age of 94.
via Chris Ellis

It did establish valuable contacts in the Balkans, Portugal and Spain, where there were right-wing regimes in power with clear Nazi sympathies, but proved remarkably unsuccessful in Britain, France and the United States. Hitler had a part in this. He initially prohibited any intelligence operations against England and the restrictions were only lifted gradually in 1936 and 1937, while espionage against the United States did not begin until the two countries went to war in December 1941. *Abteilung* III under Col Egbert von Bentivegni did score some noteworthy counter-espionage coups during the war. Between mid-1941 and October 1942, for example, it uncovered and then smashed the *Rote Kapelle* (Red Orchestra), a Europe-wide spy network run by the Soviet Union that Canaris believed had cost the lives of some 200,000 German troops due to the military intelligence its operatives had collected and transmitted by radio back to Moscow. Equally, the department's bureau chief in the Netherlands, Lt-Col Hermann Giskes, conducted the *Englandspiel* (England Game) between March 1942 and November 1943 in which foreign-born British agents were captured and turned, radioing plausible but misleading intelligence back to their controllers on the other side of the Channel. The operation, codenamed 'Nordpol' (North Pole), cost the lives of 54 other British agents, numerous Dutch resistance workers, and around 50 Royal Air Force personnel engaged in flying support missions.

However, it was *Abteilung* II that had the most aggressive role in furthering Nazi Germany's political and military ambitions, both immediately before and during World War II. Among other exploits prior to the outbreak of the conflict the department was involved in a none-too-successful disinformation campaign in Austria, where local Nazis under Artur Seyss-Inquart were demanding, and on 13 March 1938 gained, *Anschluss* (union) with Nazi Germany. More successfully, its agents promoted unrest among members of the three-million-strong *Volksdeutsche* (ethnic German) community in Czechoslovakia that was used as a pretext for Hitler's successful attempt to annex the Sudetenland region in the north and west of the country, a move that was effectively rubber-stamped by Britain and France at Munich in late September 1938. Despite the *Abwehr*'s involvement in the Czech escapade, the plan to annex the Sudetenland actually appalled Canaris as he believed, wrongly as it turned out, that the crisis would lead to a British declaration of war against Germany. For a brief period around this time he even dallied with a band of conspirators plotting to overthrow Hitler. This *Schwarze Kapelle* (Black Orchestra) comprised aristocrats, diplomats and other senior officers, including his own deputy Oster.

It was *Abteilung* II that also contained the highly secretive and specialised troops who were commonly known as Brandenburgers, men who were trained to fight in small bands in the forefront of battle and whose poorly recorded exploits, which took them to every theatre of war where German regular forces were deployed, remain shrouded in mystery. The germ of the idea for this unit dated back to the interwar period and the musings of a World War I veteran, Capt Theodore-Gottlieb von Hippel, who was subsequently to join the *Abwehr*. Like many officers in the much diminished postwar armed forces, he struggled to explain Germany's defeat in World War I and, fully expecting a second round of blood-letting, sought to uncover the means to prevent a similar outcome. Hippel's military experience during 1914–18 was in colonial East Africa, where a small force comprising no more than a few thousand German-officered local Askaris under Col Paul von Lettow-Vorbeck had outwitted much larger British-led forces and, undefeated to the end, only surrendered on 25 November 1918, when news of the Armistice finally reached them. This brilliantly conducted campaign of irregular warfare, of guerrilla-type operations, had brought significant results, not least the tying down by a comparative handful of men of thousands of enemy troops that could have been better employed elsewhere. Hippel's background with Lettow-Vorbeck made him the ideal candidate to undertake an officially sanctioned study of similar irregular operations conduct by the victorious powers, especially those of the flamboyant British officer Lt-Col T. E. Lawrence in Arabia.

Lawrence of Arabia's campaign against the Turkish forces garrisoning Arabia, Palestine and Syria between June 1916, when the British-inspired revolt by local Arabs broke out, and late October 1918, when Turkey signed an armistice, was and is regarded as a defining moment in guerrilla-style warfare. Studying the action in detail and reading Lawrence's own writings, Hippel identified several aspects of its conduct that might prove of benefit to German in any future conflict. In a strategy paralleling that of Lettow-Vorbeck, Lawrence's small force had tied down thousands of Turkish troops, had paralysed the region's scanty rail links and, unlike the totally isolated Lettow-Vorbeck, had cooperated to considerable effect with offensives by larger conventional forces,

especially during the Battle of Megiddo in September 1918. Hippel reasoned that similar forces could be employed in a conventional European war in the van of, or indeed far in advance of, an offensive. Well trained and motivated, their role would be to operate in small, highly mobile bands, to strike fast and hard at targets that were of great military value — such as enemy headquarters — or those that might be destroyed to impede attacks by regular forces, such as river or canal bridges. Stealth and surprise were vital to these hit-and-run missions, but the Brandenburgers also employed methods that came close to, and sometimes crossed, the line of internationally accepted military conduct and law. Whether by good fortune or intent Hippel's thoughts melded well with the rapidly evolving strategy of the fast-moving Blitzkrieg attacks that would bring Nazi Germany great victories between 1939 and 1941.

Hippel had the ear of Canaris, whom he considered a friend, and the *Abwehr* commander concurred with his subordinate's findings. The admiral was aware that the army's senior generals would in all likelihood oppose the formation of such a specialist unit, particularly one that was independent of them and answerable to the *Abwehr* alone, but knowing that he enjoyed Hitler's confidence and sufficient status within the OKW hierarchy, Canaris judged, correctly as events turned out, that the Brandenburgers would indeed be raised and maintained under the *Abwehr* umbrella and operate directly under the OKW. Canaris was probably less aware of the impact that simmering rivalry between the *Abwehr* and the SS, the guardians of National Socialism, would have on the fortunes of the Brandenburgers. The *Abwehr* was at heart an agency for gathering and disseminating intelligence, with each *Abteilung* having three sub-sections — air force, army and navy — and any action taken on the basis of this information was made by either the relevant branch of the armed forces or, in the case of internal security, the various local, regional and national police forces that by 1936 were effectively run by a department of the SS, the *Sicherheitsdienst* (SD/Security Service).

The SD had been founded by Heinrich Himmler in March 1934 and was responsible not only for the safety of Hitler and the wider Nazi leadership but was also tasked with safeguarding the Third Reich and National Socialism itself. Its ranks were filled with

Below: The main personnel of the *Abwehr* during the war years until it was broken up in 1944 and its duties passed over to the SS.

AMT AUSLAND/ABWEHR PERSONNEL

Commanders
Capt Konrad Patzig (1932–35)
Adm Wilhelm Canaris (1935–44)

Department	Commander	Role
Amtsgruppe Ausland	Vice-Adm Leopold Bürkner	Overt intelligence gathering
Abteilung Z	Maj-Gen Hans Oster (1938-43) Col Jakobsen (1943–44)	Administration
Abteilung I	Col Hans Piekenbrock (1937–43) Col Georg Hansen (1943–1944)	Foreign espionage
Abteilung II	Maj Helmut Groscurth (1938–39) Col Edwin Lahousen, Edler von Vivremont (1939–43) Col Wessel von Freytag-Loringhoven (1943–44)	Sabotage and subversion
Abteilung III	Maj Bamler (1933–39) Col Franz-Eccard von Bentivegni (1939-44)	Counter-espionage

Left: Admiral Wilhelm Canaris and SS-Gruppenführer Reinhard Heydrich seen before the war. From the outset there was tension between the SS and the Abwehr — although this was helped in the initial stages by the relationship between Canaris and Heydrich who had served together in the Reichsmarine.

Reinhard Tristan Eugen Heydrich was born on 7 March 1904 in Halle an der Saale, and was involved in extreme right-wing politics from an early age. A member of the Freikorps in 1919–20, in 1922 he joined the Reichsmarine, but was cashiered by a naval court in 1931 following a love affair with the daughter of a naval officer. In 1931 he joined the NSDAP and SS and was promoted by Heinrich Himmler who took him under his wing. An SS-Standartenführer by July 1932, he was promoted again to head the political department of the Munich police department in 1933 as an SS-Oberführer. He played an important part in the June 1934 'Night of the Long Knives' that disposed of Ernst Röhm and in 1936 he became chief of the Sicherheitspolizei and the Sicherheitsdienst for the whole German Reich. Three years later, Heydrich took charge of the RSHA (Department of Security). The RSHA was responsible for all official and secret police and security departments in Germany. In 1940 he became president of the International Criminal Police Commission and sought to develop spy rings in other countries — and this would bring him back into contact with Canaris again. Heydrich was fundamental to the progress of the Nazi government from anti-semitism to genocide. It was he who organised the 'concentration' of Polish Jews in ghettos and mass deportations from Germany, Austria and Poland. He chaired the Wannsee conference (20 January 1942), where the 'Final Solution' was discussed.(See also caption on page 30.)
Bundesarchiv

dedicated Nazis, not least in the person of the SD's first chief, the cold and ambitious Reinhard Heydrich. Himmler and Heydrich had already played a part in convincing Admiral Erich Raeder of the need to dismiss Patzig, an officer of the old school openly scathing about National Socialism, and were sarcastically dismissive of Raeder's choice of Canaris as his replacement, nicknaming him '*der Weihnachtsmann*' (Father Christmas) behind his back because of his white hair. Strangely Canaris and Heydrich had once been brother officers on a cruiser, the *Berlin*, until an ill-judged incident with the daughter of a shipyard director in 1931 forced the latter to resign from the service, whereupon he immediately joined the Nazi Party and shortly thereafter the SS. Promotion was rapid and in 1939 Heydrich was given command of the newly created *Reichssicherheitshauptamt* (RSHA/Reich Security Main Office), a sinister co-ordinating body of immense power that effectively controlled all of Nazi Germany's secret police.

On paper at least the *Abwehr* and SD/RSHA had clearly defined and separate areas of responsibility that should not have brought them into conflict, yet the tortuous nature of Nazi politics, not least the scheming of Himmler and other senior SS officials, ensured that relations between the heads of the *Abwehr* and SD/RSHA were at least potentially unstable, particularly as it was suspected by Himmler and Heydrich, and in some case known beyond doubt, that Canaris, Oster and other *Abwehr* members were at the very least lukewarm Nazis. Yet for a time the two bodies maintained a reasonably good working relationship and it appears that Canaris and Heydrich had a genuine friendship. In the early stages of World War II, the underlying tensions between the *Abwehr* and SD/RSHA were probably kept in check by the outstanding feats of arms of the German forces, which were undoubtedly aided by the *Abwehr* and its Brandenburgers, and the SS's unsureness as to its actual power and position within the Third Reich. Yet subsequent reversals on the battlefield, *Abwehr* intelligence failures, plotting against the Nazis by its senior figures and the eventual power of the SS combined to bring Canaris's department and its leader to their knees. Among those destined to be struck by the fallout from this struggle were the Brandenburgers themselves, but between 1939 and 1944, when Canaris and the *Abwehr* finally fell victim to the SS, they conducted some of the most daring exploits seen during the entire war.

READY FOR WAR

Below: Polish Volksdeutsche — those of German ancestry — who deserted the Polish Army to join the Nazis.

Under the direction of Col Erwin Lahousen, head of the *Abwehr's Abteilung* II, Capt Theodore von Hippel was tasked with finding the recruits who would fill the ranks of the Brandenburg detachments, which would expand with increasingly rapidity between the outbreak of war in September 1939 and the invasion of the Soviet Union in June 1941. He was looking for particular types of men: those who could demonstrate hardiness, resourcefulness and self-reliance, and those who had a useful skill that could be put to a military use. Hippel was especially interested in those who had excellent language abilities and, much to the chagrin of the SS which trumpeted its racial purity, he was willing to accept pretty much anyone who fitted the bill, particularly if they could match their language expertise with a deep understanding of the customs and colloquialisms of the country or countries concerned. Hippel recognised from the outset that it was more important for Brandenburgers to blend in with their surroundings than attain the levels of racial purity demanded of early recruits to the SS. Although none initially realised he was being interviewed for highly dangerous service with the *Abwehr* rather that the regular armed forces, there was no shortage of potential candidates, and as an additional bonus they were able to supply up-to-date official documents and passes from their homelands that could be copied and would prove immensely valuable for future operations. Many of the original recruits were *Volksdeutsche*, ethnic Germans who had grown up in the recently annexed Sudetenland or lived in Poland along its border with Germany. These men, many fluent in not only German but also Czech and Polish, were brought together in the first six months of 1939. The new unit comprised just two companies with the first having the additional title of the German Company (*Deutsche Kompanie*).

As the Brandenburgers expanded, a second source of suitable manpower was the German citizens who had left their homeland to seek their fortunes and a better life elsewhere after World War I, when the country was in economic turmoil. A large number had settled in South America and Africa, but in the late 1930s they had been encouraged to return to a newly prosperous Nazi Germany. A third pool of recruits was members of other Nordic races, such as the inhabitants of Finland, the Baltic states of Estonia, Latvia, Lithuania, and — in a decision that infuriated the SS — this included people that the latter considered racially impure. These came from the Slavic nations, including ethnic Russians opposed to their homeland's regime or those fighting against domination of their lands, such as the Ukraine, that also provided a pool of *Volksdeutche*. The Balkans also proved a useful source of men as did Nazi sympathisers spread across the nations of Western Europe. These original recruits, and all subsequent Brandenburgers, underwent intense training to learn techniques beyond those thought relevant to the ordinary soldier. Among the specialist skills taught by instructors were those appropriate for urban guerrillas and partisans operating in the countryside. Emphasis was placed on small unit skills, tracking and navigation and survival skills. As the scope for Brandenburger operations widened, these courses would be supplemented by parachute training, maritime skills and skiing. Unlike regular army units the Brandenburgers trained with live ammunition like their counterparts in the Waffen-SS. Recruits were also sent on several courses at Gut Quensee, a school established by the *Abwehr* outside Berlin to train its agents.

The first opportunity to test the validity of the Brandenburger concept and the effectiveness of the training programme came with Hitler's decision to invade Poland. Although they belonged to a comparatively new and untried outfit, the soon-to-be-Brandenburgers were given a leading and top-secret role in plans for the invasion, which was codenamed '*Fall Weiss*' (Case White). Canaris was ordered to put his men not already active in Poland on 48-hour standby on the evening of 24 August, the day after Hitler had gained the Soviet Union's acquiescence to the invasion of their mutual neighbour through the signing of a non-aggression pact. Details of the subsequent operations remain sketchy but it is known that *Abwehr* sections in three military districts in the eastern Third Reich, at Breslau and Königsberg in Germany proper and a third based in the Austrian capital of Vienna, were ordered to send an estimated 16 Brandenburger teams of *Volksdeutche* from the Sudetenland and Poland into Polish territory before the start of the invasion. The Breslau and Vienna groups were partly charged with seizing key economic targets in eastern Poland, chiefly the coal and iron ore mines of Polish Silesia, to prevent their destruction and loss to the Nazi economy. They

Above: Hitler visits the Schöber Line during the occupation of the Sudetenland. Brandenburgers were involved in Czechoslovakia to ensure that key bridges and crossroads were kept clear for the invading German troops. *Bundesarchiv*

infiltrated these installations well before the outbreak of hostilities, stashed their weapons and took jobs as ordinary Polish workers. Closer to the invasion date members of teams codenamed 'Bisek' and 'Georgey' were dressed in Polish uniforms or civilian clothes and smuggled in high explosives intending to neutralise military targets. Brandenburgers from Königsberg in east Prussia were tasked with seizing vital bridges over the Vistula River, a key defensive line north of the Polish capital Warsaw, to prevent their destruction before the arrival of spearheads of Gen Fodor von Bock's Army Group North.

Perhaps the most significant purely military role of the ground war for the Brandenburgers was given to the group of some 34 men commanded by 2-Lt Hans-Albrecht Herzner. These were ordered to take the Jablunkov Pass in the Beskid Mountains through which ran the railway line linking Polish Silesia to German-controlled eastern Czechoslovakia. It was a vital corridor for the invasion and two divisions from Gen Wilhelm List's Fourteenth Army stood ready to drive through the pass to take the city of Cracow in the opening days of the campaign, thereby protecting the eastern flank of the main drive by Gen Gerd von Rundstedt's Army Group South on Warsaw. Herzner's men, who were mostly Polish *Volksdeutsche*, launched their cross-border attack in the early hours of 26 August in accordance with the original timetable for Case White. They caught the larger Polish garrison by surprise; there was some fierce fighting around the station at Mosty but the Poles eventually surrendered. Then one of their officers informed a puzzled Herzner that Germany and Poland were not actually at war, a fact confirmed when the lieutenant was able to contact his frantic *Abwehr* superior at Zilina in Slovakia. It appears that Hitler had a temporary loss of nerve on the eve of the attack, chiefly because on the 25th the British and Polish authorities had signed a mutual assistance pact that pledged either to come to the aid of the other if attacked by what was termed a European power but meant Germany. Canaris had attempted to halt the attack on the pass when informed of Hitler's *volte face* but Herzner lacked a radio to receive the recall order.

Below right: Hitler and Keitel. Keitel turned down Canaris's recommendation that Herzner receive the Iron Cross for storming the Jablunkov Pass.

Below: The Polish campaign: note Gleiwitz and the Jablunkov Pass in Polish Silesia.

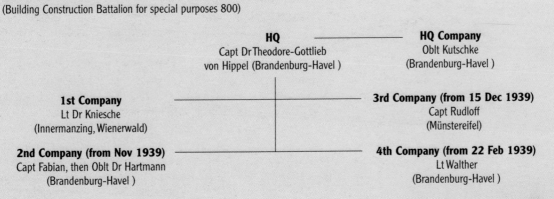

BAU-LEHR-BATAILLON zbV 800 DECEMBER 1939–MAY 1940
(Building Construction Battalion for special purposes 800)

HQ ———————— **HQ Company**
Capt Dr Theodore-Gottlieb Oblt Kutschke
von Hippel (Brandenburg-Havel) (Brandenburg-Havel)

1st Company **3rd Company (from 15 Dec 1939)**
Lt Dr Kniesche Capt Rudloff
(Innermanzing, Wienerwald) (Münstereifel)

2nd Company (from Nov 1939) **4th Company (from 22 Feb 1939)**
Capt Fabian, then Oblt Dr Hartmann Lt Walther
(Brandenburg-Havel) (Brandenburg-Havel)

Despite this comedy of errors at the front, it took little time for Hitler to regain his nerve and on the night of 31 August, members of the SS acting on Reinhard Heydrich's orders engineered a border incident centred on a small radio station at Gleiwitz — in Germany but just one mile (1.6km) from the Polish frontier — as a pretext to launch the invasion. Dressed in Polish uniforms allegedly provided by the unknowing *Abwehr*, eight men under SS Maj Alfred Naujocks, a member of the SD, attacked the station, fired a few shots — picked up by its German listeners — to subdue its small staff, and began broadcasting in Polish that it was time for Poland to invade Germany. To add veracity to the ruse, Naujocks' team killed a concentration camp inmate they had brought with them dressed in a Polish uniform. Exposed for the scrutiny of the media, the wider world had little time to react to this stage-managed event for on the morning of 1 September German troops stormed into Poland and the remaining Brandenburger teams set about their various tasks. Few details are available of these operations but the coal and iron ore mines of Silesia were captured with only limited damage and units of Army Group North began crossing the Vistula with little difficulty five days after the opening of the campaign. Poland was effectively defeated with a matter of days and Warsaw surrendered on the 27th.

The Polish campaign had mostly proved the validity of Hippel's concept yet the Brandenburgers received little tangible official recognition for their efforts. Canaris did request that Herzner receive the Iron Cross for the somewhat premature storming of the Jablunkov Pass but was turned down by Gen Wilhelm Keitel, head of the OKW, on the grounds that the medal was only awarded during wartime and that Germany and Poland were not actually at war when the action at Jablunkov took place. However, the unit did receive a new title on 25 October, becoming the *Lehr und Bau Kompanie zbV 800* (Special Duty Training and Construction Company No 800). The newly activated command remained under Hippel and was established at Brandenburg-an-der-Havel for the first time. Its men began to refer to their unit as the Brandenburg Company and to themselves as Brandenburgers.

Poland had proved the Brandenburgers' value and in the latter part of 1939 the unit grew significantly so that on 15 December it was retitled *Bau-Lehr-Bataillon zbV 800*. Elements of the four-company battalion made their debut in Western Europe during the invasion of Denmark and Norway, which opened on 9 April 1940. Information is sketchy but it appears Danish-speaking Brandenburgers dressed as local soldiers captured crossings over the Grosse Belt, thereby allowing regular troops to drive into the north of the country. Similar ploys were also used by a Brandenburg detachment known as the *Nordzug* (North Platoon) during the first stages of the two-month campaign to subdue

Further units were also added within the battalion and later integrated within the unit:

Motorcycle platoon
Oblt Erwin Graf Thun

Paratrooper Platoon
Lt Dlab

North Platoon (Recovery Platoon)
Lt Zülch

West Platoon
Sgt Kürschner

Southeast Company

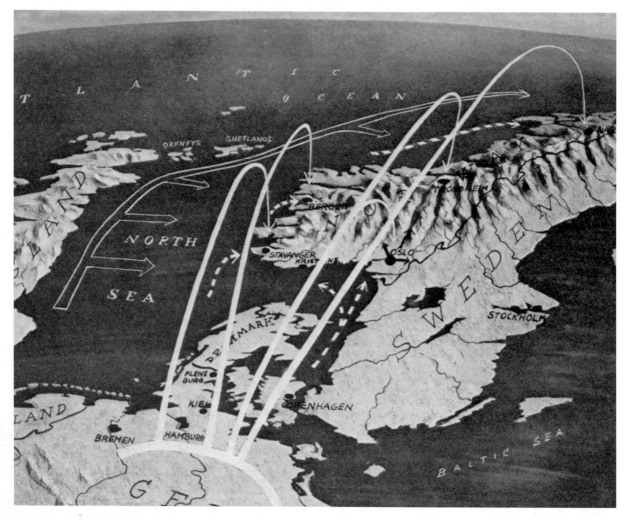

Above: This map, taken from the propaganda magazine *Signal*, shows the Nazi view of the invasion of Denmark and Norway from 9 April 1940. 'The most important points,' the article announced, 'were occupied like lightning by German troops. At the same time German forces took over the defence of Denmark against any attempts at invasion by the English.'

Norway. On 20 April it left Brandenburg for Oslo by train and was deployed to sabotage Norwegian communications. On 1 May, one of the *Nordzug*'s units flew from Trondheim to support the drive on Namsos by the 181st Infantry Division. Norway surrendered on 12 June and the *Nordzug* departed eight days later.

The campaigns in Poland, Denmark and Norway thus established a pattern that was repeated in subsequent Brandenburg operations. First, a decision was taken by the *Abwehr*'s *Abteilung* II as to whether the troops involved should wear disguises or not. Second, the extent of the disguise was settled: was it to be partial (*Halbtarnung*/semi-camouflage) with perhaps just a few items — a greatcoat and helmet, say — or should those involved go further and adopt the whole panoply of enemy's military clothing (*Volltarnung*/full camouflage)? Third, details were passed down to the relevant Brandenburger group in the field, which would determine the size of the detachment it would commit to the operation, usually between a mere handful of men to a platoon depending on the target's importance. The lessons learned by the Brandenburgers in Denmark and Norway undoubtedly proved invaluable during the main event in Western Europe — 'Fall Gelb' (Case Yellow), the invasion of France and the Low Countries. Even before the outbreak of hostilities disguised Brandenburgers had been infiltrated into the Benelux countries to photograph and sketch potential targets, make contact with pro-Nazi sympathisers and acquire second-hand military clothing.

IN ACTION

BLITZKRIEG IN THE WEST

Fall Gelb opened at 0535 hours on 10 May with a massive attack into northern Belgium and the Netherlands by the two armies of Gen Fedor von Bock's Army Group B. This forced the Anglo-French units to move forward from their positions along the border between France and Belgium in order to meet the developing threat. Part of Army Group B, Gen Walter von Reichenau's Sixth Army, was ordered to 'advance on the line Venlo–Aachen, to cross the Meuse [in German, Maas] quickly and to pass through the Belgian defence system without delay'. To ensure that von Reichenau's forces and those of Gen der Artillerie Georg von Küchler's Eighteenth Army to the north were able to push forward at utmost speed, some 500 Brandenburgers were tasked with capturing intact key river and canal bridges. If destroyed, the momentum of the offensive would be seriously reduced.

The various Brandenburg detachments had several missions and most wore *Halbtarnung.* For example, four bridges over the Juliana Canal at Berg, Obbicht, Urmond and Stein were taken intact by 2-Lt Kürschner's *Westzug* (West Platoon) so that the 7th Infantry Division could move into Holland; between Elsenborn and St. Vith the 3rd Company took 19 out of 24 targets that had been assigned to it. However, not all of the Brandenburger operations were successful: on 10 May 2-Lt Siegfried Grabert's 2nd Platoon of the 4th Company only took one of the four bridges assigned to it; three others, those at Maaseyck over the Juliana Canal and two over the Meuse at Roermond, were destroyed.

One of the most spectacular missions was that of the 4th Company's 1st Platoon under Lt Wilhelm Walther. The 450-yard (410m) Gennep bridge, which carried the rail line running from

Below: Capt Hans-Jürgen Rudloff inspects his troops of the IIIrd Battalion after the French campaign during training for Operation 'Sealion'. *Bundesarchiv*

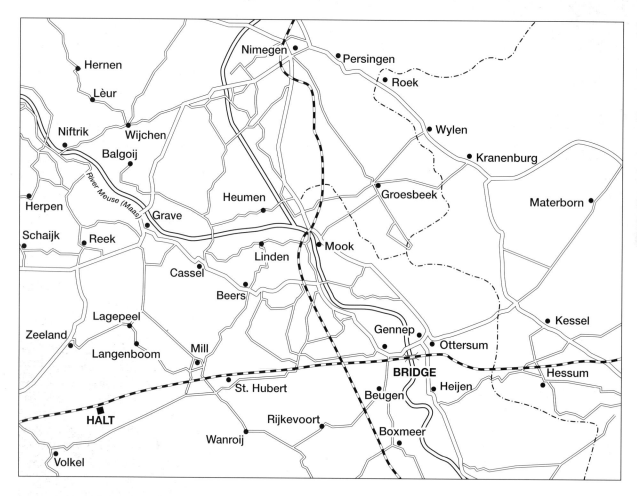

Above: Gennep railway bridge crosses the Meuse (Maas) west of the town. The halt at which the train stopped is identified between Uden and St Hubert.

Above right: Gennep railway bridge. *Bundesarchiv*

Right: The bridges over the Meuse (Maas), Albert and Juliana canals that were among the highest priorities for the German advance. Note Eben Emael at the bottom, captured by a glider-borne assault. Four bridges over the Juliana Canal at Berg, Obbicht, Urmond and Stein were taken intact by 2-Lt Kürschner's *Westzug* (West Platoon)

Goch in Germany into Holland (no longer running today), was little more than two miles (3km) from the Dutch-German border. It was of particular importance as its capture would not only permit German regular forces to cut westward through the Dutch defensive position — known as the Peel Line — before it could be properly manned, thereby splitting Holland in two, but also bring relief to the scattered paratrooper units that had landed at various points around Rotterdam and the Hague at the outbreak of the invasion. The platoon and a number of Dutch Nazis began moving to the target several hours before the main assault, crossing the Dutch border at 2330 hours on 9 May. Under cover of darkness a small party moved undetected through the low-lying ground between the Niers river and the railway embankment, crossed the road running between Heijen and Gennep, and then took cover among the scrub that covered the banks of the Meuse near the target bridge.

Shortly before dawn, some 10 minutes before main invasion began, one of four Dutch military policemen at the bridge's eastern end spied six figures — two were wearing the same uniform as the guard while the four others, less identifiable, were cloaked in long overcoats — calmly moving towards him. He and two colleagues, confused by the strange scene, were quickly overpowered as was a fourth policeman manning a telephone. One of the Brandenburgers, a fluent Dutch-speaker, now rang the western guardhouse of the bridge and reported that he had four prisoners on his hands and was sending them across for interrogation along with two guards. An exchange was made in the middle of the bridge with the four prisoners being marched off to a

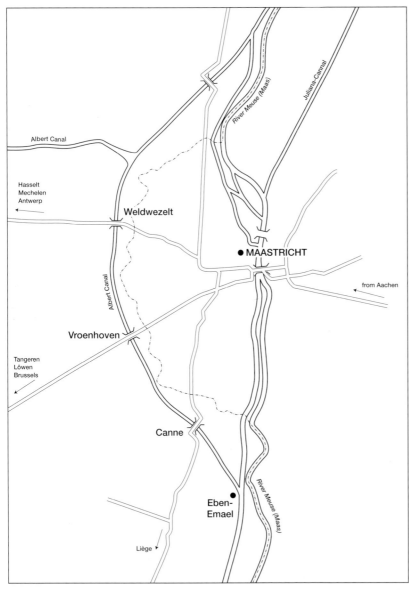

COLONEL G. J. SAS

It was a bizarre paradox that the high-risk operations conducted by the Brandenburger on 10 May 1940, during the opening phase of Fall Weiss, were very nearly compromised by one of the *Abwehr*'s own most senior figures. Col Hans Oster was Adm Wilhelm Canaris's deputy and the two men had some involvement in a plot to remove Hitler from power. Canaris was the more cautious of the two; Oster willing to take much greater risks to undermine the Nazis' war plans for the conquest of Western Europe.

Sas was the Dutch military attaché in Berlin and had regular contact with Oster. In April it appears that Oster told Sas of Hitler's imminent attacks on Denmark and Norway, information that was passed on to the Danish ambassador. On 3 May the two men met again and Oster revealed that in all likelihood both the Netherlands and Belgium would be attacked in the very near future. Finally, over dinner on the 9th Oster stated categorically that the Low Countries were to be attacked at dawn the following day. Sas hurried away and telephoned the Dutch War Office. The conversation was brief and Sas spoke the code number 210 — 200 meant the invasion of Holland and 10 referred to the date. Sas's reports of German intentions had previously been mostly discounted and later that night the head of Dutch intelligence service telephoned Sas to confirm his previous conversation. He did so, but the information was never acted upon.

The Sas affair certainly had not gone unnoticed in Germany as his conversations on the 9th had been picked up by the Nazi security services. Oster's name had not been mentioned but they were clear that Sas's information could have only come from a senior figure, one likely to be serving in the intelligence services. The *Abwehr*, the Brandenburgers parent body, was for the first of several times brought under suspicion.

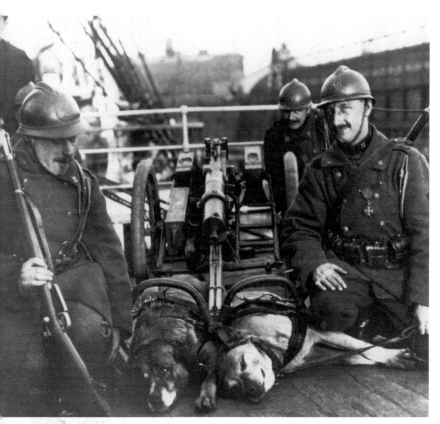

guardhouse at its western end after a perfunctory search that failed to uncover the weapons they were carrying. Only one Dutch military policemen was now left in the middle of the bridge and the two disguised Brandenburgers returned to its eastern end. The lone Dutch sentry next spotted a train approaching from the direction of the German border but no immediate action was taken when he telephoned the information back to his superior, an aged sergeant, at the western end. German troops from the train overpowered the sentry before he could detonate the explosive charges that had been placed on the bridge. The bridge was captured intact although a few Dutch troops on the west bank did open fire briefly. They were forced to surrender when they were caught in a crossfire from the four Brandenburger prisoners who had overpowered their guards in the confusion of the train's approach and their colleagues at the eastern end of the bridge. The Brandenburgers' coup allowed the 9th Panzer Division to push forward rapidly.

Above: The Brandenburgers donned Belgian overcoats — as exemplified in this splendid photograph — to cover their uniforms. (The machine gun is a Belgian Maxim 7.65 and the rifles are 1889 Mausers.) *via George Forty*

After the successes of 10 May, the Brandenburgers were temporarily withdrawn from the action and sent on leave but at the end of the month their services were called upon once more. The German high command had always feared that their lightning attacks might be delayed in the Low Countries by either the Dutch or Belgians opening the sluice gates of their extensive networks of drainage canals and thereby flooding the surrounding low-lying countryside and making it impassable to German forces. Such an event had already taken place around Nieuport on the Flanders coast and it appeared that a similar fate awaited the sluice gates on the Yser River. Grabert and 12 other Brandenburgers on leave in Germany were ordered to Ghent at short notice and were informed that they had to seize the pump houses on the south bank of the Yser near the Ostend–Nieuport road bridge. With their uniforms hidden under captured Belgian Army greatcoats and benefiting from the confused and fluid situation along the Allied front line Grabert's men headed for Ostend from Ghent in a captured Belgian military bus. At Ostend a French-speaking Brandenburger discovered from a Belgian officer that his army had surrendered and that the British were in control of Nieuport and the bridge. Speed was of the essence as the British were likely to blow both the bridge and the sluice gates to cover their ongoing evacuation from the beaches at Dunkirk a few miles along the coast

The 15-mile (24km) journey to the objective from Ostend passed without a hitch, although the Brandenburgers' rate of progress was slowed by the long straggling columns of refugees they encountered. Nevertheless at around 1900 hours on the 27th they reached their target only to be hit by intense fire from British positions on the far side of the river. Grabert's team quickly debussed, removed their Belgian overcoats and made for a piece of dead ground just 50 yards (45m) from the bridge that sheltered then from the fire. Here they waited until nightfall and then Grabert and a corporal, Janovsky, who was to be awarded the Iron Cross for his part in the unfolding drama, crawled forward, freezing frequently to avoid being revealed under the glare of illuminating Very lights, and began dismantling the explosive charges they uncovered as they made their way to the opposite end of the bridge. Once across, and with the charges disarmed, Grabert signalled the other Brandenburgers to join him. A vicious close-quarters firefight developed in the darkness but the Brandenburgers were able to beat the British away from the bridge and secure the undamaged pump houses until relieved by other German units. The Brandenburgers did suffer casualties during the attack but had secured a vital bridge and prevented the flooding of the area.

The Brandenburgers had undoubtedly performed well during the initial invasion. Twenty-four hours after it had opened Hippel recorded that 42 out of 61 Brandenburger operations had succeeded. One of his men, Walther, was subsequently awarded the Knight's Cross — the unit's first — and 120 other Brandenburgers received various grades of the Iron Cross.

From May 1940 the Brandenburgers had been earmarked for considerable expansion. The original battalion was to be expanded threefold to regimental strength and as of 15 May it was decreed that the new *Lehr Regiment Brandenburg zbV 800* would be split with each of its three battalions having separate bases and areas of operations. While the staff were based in Berlin itself, the Ist Battalion under Hippel was earmarked for overseas operations and was to be stationed in nearby Brandenburg, the IInd Battalion was to be deployed to Baden-Unterwaltersdorf, Austria, for service in eastern or southeastern Europe, while the IIIrd Battalion was to establish a base at Aachen (later Düren) in the Rhineland for missions in western, northern and southern Europe. The regimental commander was named as Maj Kewisch. However, the implementation of these structural changes was delayed by ongoing military events and not fully completed until April 1941.

Above: What happened when the bridges weren't captured intact. The advance would continue but without heavy weapons or armoured vehicles — major components of Blitzkrieg. *via George Forty*

'SEALION' AND 'FELIX' — THE CANCELLED OPERATIONS

Paris was formally occupied on 14 June and the French agreed an armistice with Germany on the 22nd. England, militarily weak despite the successful evacuation from the Dunkirk beaches, now seemed ripe for invasion and on 16 July Hitler issued his Directive No 16 which related to 'preparations for a landing operation against England'. In its final form the assault, codenamed '*Seelöwe*' (Sealion), called for major landings along the coast of southeast England by elements of Army Group A, mostly based in the Pas de Calais region of northeast France. Two Brandenburger units were earmarked for

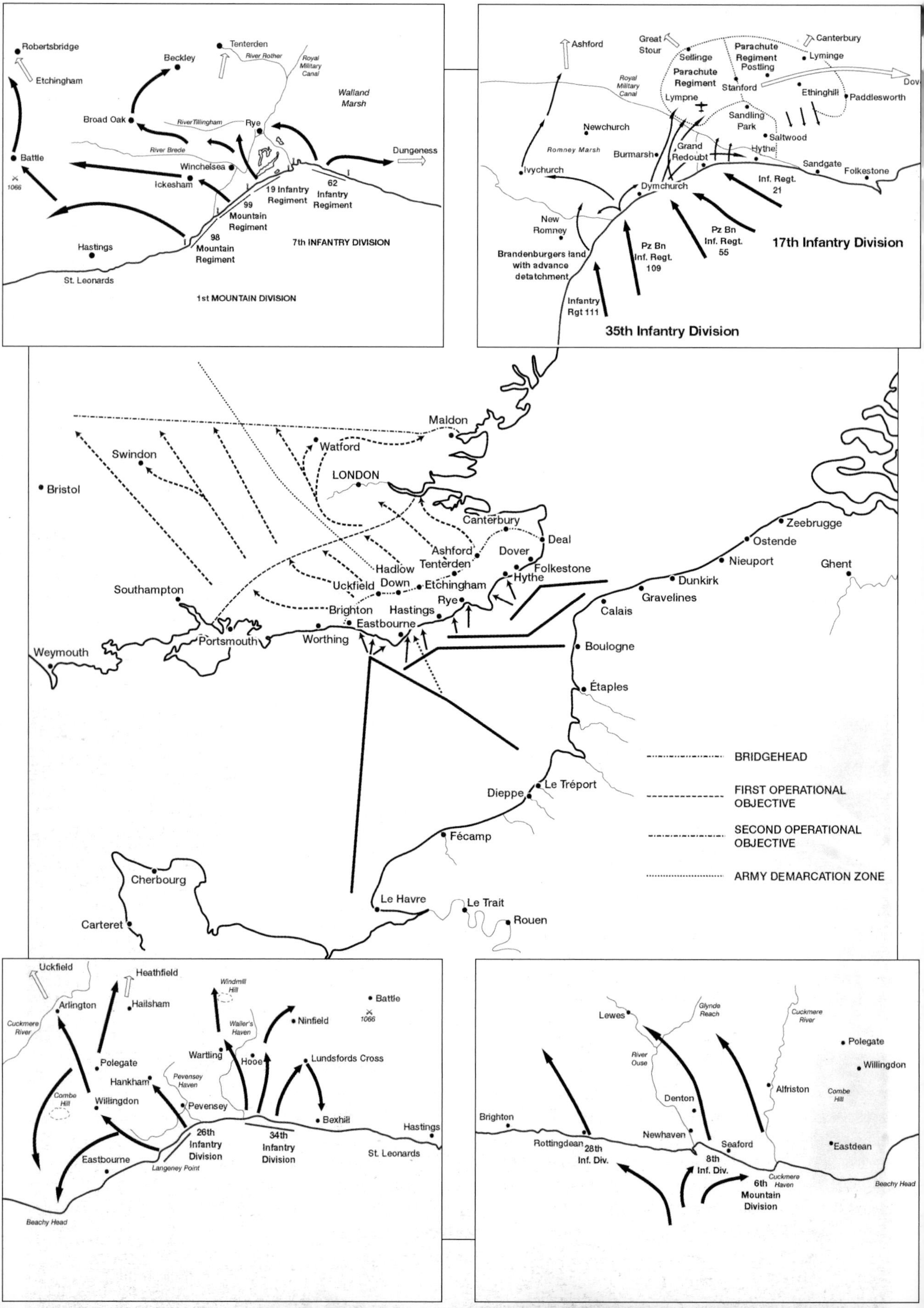

Robertsbridge
Etchingham
Battle
1066
Tenterden
River Rother
Royal Military Canal
Beckley
Walland Marsh
Broad Oak
River Tillingham
Rye
River Brede
Dungeness
Winchelsea
Ickesham
19 Infantry Regiment
62 Infantry Regiment
99 Mountain Regiment
98 Mountain Regiment
7th INFANTRY DIVISION
Hastings
St. Leonards
1st MOUNTAIN DIVISION
Ashford
Great Stour
Canterbury
Sellinge
Parachute Regiment
Parachute Regiment Postling
Lyminge
Royal Military Canal
Stanford
Ethinghill
Paddlesworth
Lympne
Newchurch
Sandling Park
Saltwood
Romney Marsh
Burmarsh
Grand Redoubt
Hythe
Sandgate
Folkestone
Ivychurch
Dymchurch
Inf. Regt. 21
New Romney
Pz Bn Inf. Regt. 55
Pz Bn Inf. Regt. 109
17th Infantry Division
Brandenburgers land with advance detatchment
Infantry Rgt 111
35th Infantry Division
Maldon
Watford
Swindon
LONDON
Bristol
Canterbury
Deal
Ashford
Dover
Tenterden
Hadlow Down
Folkestone
Hythe
Zeebrugge
Ostende
Nieuport
Ghent
Dunkirk
Gravelines
Calais
Southampton
Uckfield
Etchingham
Rye
Brighton
Hastings
Eastbourne
Portsmouth
Worthing
Weymouth
Boulogne
Étaples
BRIDGEHEAD
FIRST OPERATIONAL OBJECTIVE
SECOND OPERATIONAL OBJECTIVE
ARMY DEMARCATION ZONE
Le Tréport
Dieppe
Fécamp
Cherbourg
Carteret
Le Havre
Le Trait
Rouen
Uckfield
Heathfield
Windmill Hill
Battle
Arlington
Hailsham
Cuckmere River
Waller's Haven
Ninfield
1066
Wartling
Hooe
Lundsfords Cross
Polegate
Hankham
Pevensey Haven
Combe Hill
Willingdon
Pevensey
Bexhill
Hastings
26th Infantry Division
34th Infantry Division
St. Leonards
Eastbourne
Langeney Point
Beachy Head
Lewes
Glynde Reach
Cuckmere River
Polegate
River Ouse
Willingdon
Alfriston
Denton
Combe Hill
Brighton
Newhaven
Seaford
Rottingdean
28th Inf. Div.
8th Inf. Div.
Eastdean
Cuckmere Haven
6th Mountain Division
Beachy Head

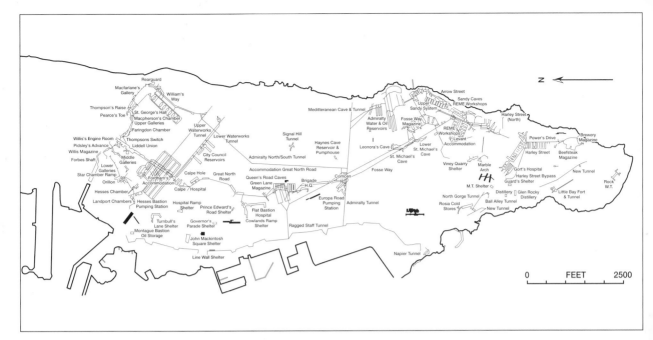

Left: Peter Schenk's analysis of the invasion plans for Operation 'Sealion' provides a blueprint of the German intentions (see page 95). The Brandenburgers of Ist and IIIrd Battalions were intended to play key roles, the former with Sixteenth Army, the latter the Ninth. Two units were allocated to 34th and 26th Infantry Divisions and were tasked with the destruction of the gun battery at Beachy Head and a nearby radio station. Two more platoons were to be with 35th Infantry Division and were tasked with the neutralisation of bases on the coast and Royal Military Canal. The most important mission was that of 4th Company — to destroy Dover Harbour's coastal batteries and prevent the harbour mouth from being blocked to the invasion fleet.

Above and Below: Operation 'Felix' planned an invasion of Gibraltar via Spain. Hitler's War Directive No 18 of 12 November 1940 laid out the ground rules, and the detailed plan called for over 65,000 men and 13,000 tons of ammunition including some 20,000 shells to silence the British batteries. With a garrison of 10,000, miles of underground tunnels (**Above**) and sufficient provisions for an 18-month siege, Gibraltar was no pushover, and Spanish co-operation was essential. However, Franco (**Below**) seen meeting Hitler on 23 October 1940 at Hendaye in southwest France (see page 24); did not agree to it, preferring to rebuild his country that had already been shattered by a protracted civil war. Hitler, his eye taken by the Italian attack on Greece and planning for 'Barbarossa', quietly shelved the idea. *IWM MH11546*

'Sealion' and, after training on the island of Helgoland, Hippel's Ist Battalion moved to the assembly point of Army Group A's Sixteenth Army just to the east of Dunkirk, while Capt Hans-Jürgen Rudloff's IIIrd Battalion assembled farther south in Normandy, close to Caen, for service with the Sixth Army. The units were tasked with specific missions: half of Hippel's men were to destroy some port facilities at Folkestone while the remainder neutralised the large rail guns that had been identified at Dungeness; the IIIrd Battalion was to make a diversionary landing to capture Weymouth to lure British forces away from major landings at Portsmouth and Plymouth. A third contingent of English-speaking Brandenburgers was attached to the Ninth Army. These were scheduled to land with the first wave wearing British uniforms and then use motorcycles to push inland rapidly to conduct various sabotage missions. 'Sealion' was an opportunity lost and never came to fruition, however, as the Luftwaffe's defeat in the Battle of Britain and Hitler's growing focus on war with the Soviet Union ensured that Germany's military resources — and the Brandenburgers — would be sent to the east.

Despite the cancellation of 'Sealion', Hitler still intended to deliver a crippling blow to Britain's war effort and on 12 November issued a directive relating to a proposed operation, codenamed 'Felix', that was to drive the British from the western Mediterranean. The aim was to persuade Spanish dictator Francisco Franco either to join the Axis alliance or to allow German troops onto his soil and then capture the strategically vital naval base of Gibraltar. Fluent Spanish-speaking Canaris, who was well-known to the Spanish leader and may have proposed 'Felix' to Hitler, had initiated preparations for the mission in early July, when he and Col Piekenbrock, the head of the *Abwehr*'s *Abteilung* I, held a meeting in Madrid with Capt Hans-Jürgen Rudloff. Canaris informed the officer that when the political preparations for 'Felix' were completed part of his battalion would be transported secretly across Spain and outside Gibraltar link up with engineers and artillery detachments that had sailed from ports in southern France. Following a brief bombardment Rudloff's Brandenburgers were to storm the British fortress relying on speed and surprise. Rudloff was not altogether impressed with the risky plan but agreed to travel to Spain to observe the objective.

His mission proved worthless as Hitler, who met Franco at Hendaye in southwest France on 23 October and discussed 'Felix', grew increasing doubtful that he could draw Spain into the Axis alliance. Franco argued repeatedly at Hendaye and in subsequent discussions that his country was still recovering from its recent civil war and would not be strong enough to side with the Axis for at least two years. Equally, he was unwilling to allow German troops transit through his supposedly neutral country as it would likely precipitate declarations of war on Spain. Hitler subsequently drew up secret plans for a military occupation of Spain and considered implementing them until mid-1943 but Operation 'Felix' was officially suspended within a month of the original directive of 12 November being issued.

THE BALKANS AND 'BARBAROSSA'

German influence in and domination of Romania ensured that Hitler had a free hand within a country where Ion Antonescu, prime minister from September 1940 and effective dictator from late January 1941, was pro-Nazi and willing to bend to his wishes. Canaris secured an agreement with his counterpart in the Siguranza, the Romanian

Below: Major Wilhelm Walther in Greece, 1943, as CO of the Brandenburg Division's 1st Regiment.

intelligence service, for Germany to take over the security for much of the country's economy, chiefly its oil-producing facilities around Ploesti which were vital to Germany and likely to be a target of British sabotage squads. In October 1939 60 Brandenburgers from the 5th Company entered Romania in small groups and carried out several undercover operations to combat British sabotage efforts and they were joined in November by the 6th Company.

The Brandenburgers next military operation was at the forefront of Hitler's onslaught in the Balkans, which was prompted from October 1940 by the likely failure of the Italian offensive against Greece and the need to protect the southern flank of Operation 'Barbarossa', the forthcoming invasion of the Soviet Union. Units from the IInd Battalion saw action on 6 April 1941, the first day of Operation 'Punishment', the invasion of Yugoslavia. They were deployed, some dressed as Serbian civilians, to capture the so-called Iron Gate, a 62.5-mile (100km) long gorge on the Danube river that meanders along the border of southwest Romania and northeast Yugoslavia, to ensure that it would remain open to German traffic. (Interestingly, it was dammed in 1977 and today in parts of the Iron Gate the depth of the Danube exceeds 165yd/150m.) Men from the battalion's 8th Company under Grabert dressed in Yugoslav uniforms and successfully secured a vital bridge across the Vardar River to the west of Axiopoulos for the 2nd Panzer Division, while troops of the 5th and 7th Companies used assault boats to spearhead the crossing of the Danube near Osova. Yugoslavia surrendered on the 17th. Brandenburgers saw action in the subsequent invasion of Greece but most detachments had left the country by May.

Above: Brandenburgers dressed in Russian uniforms. *TRH Pictures*

Below: In Russia, as in the Blitzkrieg in the west, the Brandenburgers' main targets were bridges — this one over the Dvina River in Latvia was seized on 26–28 June by Oberleutnant Siegfried Grabert's 8th Company. *Bundesarchiv*

Opposite, above: Operations in the Crimea and Caucasus. Note Maikop at the bottom centre of the map.

Opposite below: Brandenburg operation against the rail line to Murmansk by the 'Hettinger' Company, August 1942, a raid discussed in Eric Lefevre's book on the division (see page 94). It was a successful raid that earned the Brandenburgers the warmest praise from Lapland Army commander Gen Eduard Dietl. The men crossed 100 miles (160km) of poor terrain, survived a Russian ambush and cut the railway line in a mission that kept them behind enemy lines for nearly two weeks.

Below: Operation 'Barbarossa'.

After the Balkans campaign the Brandenburgers were earmarked for a leading role in Operation 'Barbarossa', which officially opened at dawn on 22 June. The understrength regiment was split into three-company battalions and mostly assigned to the three army groups that had been positioned along the Soviet border. Maj Heinz's Ist Battalion companies fought with Army Group South, the IInd Battalion under Maj Paul Jacobi served with Army Group North and South, and Capt Franz Jacobi's IIIrd Battalion mostly served with Army Group Centre.

Some detachments were already within Soviet territory and many were disguised in Red Army uniforms that the Finns had captured during the Winter War of November 1939–March 1940. The Finns also provided Soviet weapons and transport to add to the veracity of the ruse. The Brandenburgers were involved in scores of clandestine operations involving the capture of bridges and crossroads to speed the Blitzkrieg and also cut telephone and telegraph lines to add to the Red Army's state of confusion. Scores of these operations took place all along the front. Typical of these was the seizure of eight bridges by the IIIrd Battalion's 10th Company to open the way for the armoured spearheads of Army Group Centre. Commanded by Lt Aretz, the company split into eight teams and, with Russian blouses over their own tunics, the men set off by truck for their targets in advance of the main attack. The greater part of the regiment was withdrawn from the Eastern Front between August and October, although two units, the 6th and 9th Companies from the IInd and IIIrd Battalions respectively remained there, fighting in the Crimea and against partisans until the following summer.

LATER OPERATIONS ON THE EASTERN FRONT

In the early summer of 1942 virtually the whole regiment was deployed to the Ukraine to spearhead the twin-pronged drive into the Caucasus and toward Stalingrad. Most of the regiment's battalions served with Army Group A, which was tasked with securing the oilfields of the Caucasus after crossing the Don River. Once again the various companies were used in a spearhead role to seize vital bridges, especially across the Don River, when the offensive began on 28 June. One of the most important was that undertaken by the IIIrd Battalion's 8th Company in support of a push by the 5th SS Panzer Division 'Wiking', the 16th

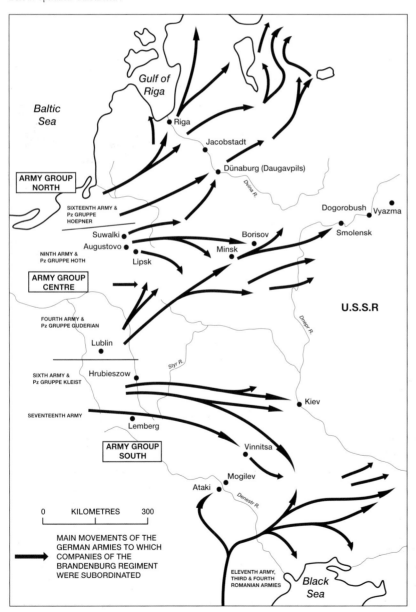

Motorised Infantry Division and the 13th Panzer Division to take the city of Maikop, an important oil-producing centre on the Kuban steppes in the northern Caucasus in August. The Brandenburgers had two detachments involved. One was a 63-man team, including many fluent Russian speakers, under Lt Baron Adrian von Foelkersam. It was to precede the attack by a long-range mission to Maikop, while a short-range operation by a single platoon under Lt Ernst Prohaska, another native Russian speaker, was tasked with seizing a bridge over the Bjelaja River across which the regular forces had to pass.

The Foelkersam detachment moved first. Dressed in NKVD uniforms they crossed the front line near Alexandrovskaja under cover of darkness on the 2nd, a week before the main attack opened, and successfully reached Maikop, where they were greeted warmly by the local NKVD commander and given billets. Over the following days, Foelkersam was taken on guided tours of the city's main installation and laid plans for a takeover. On the day of the attack, the 8th, his force split into three groups. One severed telephones and telegraph lines from Maikop to front-line units and then occupied the central telegraph office, answering any calls with the 'official' order that the city had to be abandoned. A second group under Foelkersam himself took over a strongpoint and issued false withdrawal orders to Red Army units in the immediate vicinity, while the third group succeeded in preventing the destruction of all but one of the city's oil storage tanks. On the 9th Prohaska led his team, also dressed in enemy uniforms and mounted on Red Army trucks, across the Bjelaja bridge. The appearance of apparently retreating Soviet troops sowed panic among the defenders of the bridge and, as they fled, the Brandenburgers disarmed the explosive charges that had been primed for its demolition. A spearhead from the 13th Panzer Division crossed safely and Maikop fell the same day. Foelkersam and Prohaska were both awarded the Knight's Cross for the operation, the latter posthumously.

Although the bulk of the regiment was fighting in the far south of the Eastern Front for most of 1942, some Brandenburgers saw service in the far north. The 15th Company under Lt Trommsodorf was dispatched to Finland in January to serve under Gen Eduard Dietl and established a camp near Rovaniemi. After a period of acclimatisation,

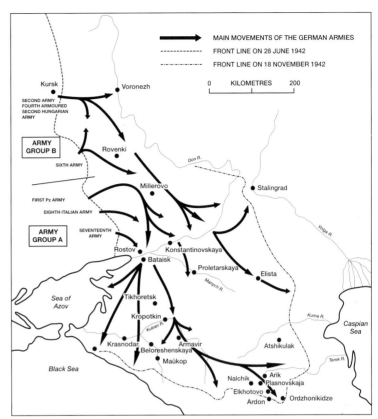

Right: The 'Desert Fox' wasn't keen at first, but the Brandenburgers soon won his approval. The first Brandenburg units —1st and 2nd Companies of the IIIrd Battalion of Lehr-Regiment Brandenburg z.b.V. 800 —arrived in North Africa in June 1941 tasked with reconnaissance duties. Redesignated Sonderverband 287, the Brandenburgers were subordinated to Sonderstab F commanded by Gen der Flieger Felmy until Koenen arrived to take command. *via George Forty*

Below: Operation 'Salaam', the planned insertion of German agents into Cairo.

the so-called Trommsodorf Company joined a battle group that included German mountain troops and a Finnish detachment. The group's operation in late March–early April was to sever Russian supply lines running between Leningrad and Murmansk, the ice-free port, but the raid ended in failure and the Brandenburgers returned to base. Trommsodorf left — as did his replacement — and in mid-April a new officer, Lt Hettinger, arrived. After weeks of intensive training, his Hettinger Company embarked on another raid against the Leningrad–Murmansk Line on 3 August — the objective lay 100 miles (160km) behind the front line. After setting off from Kairala, the company lived partly off the

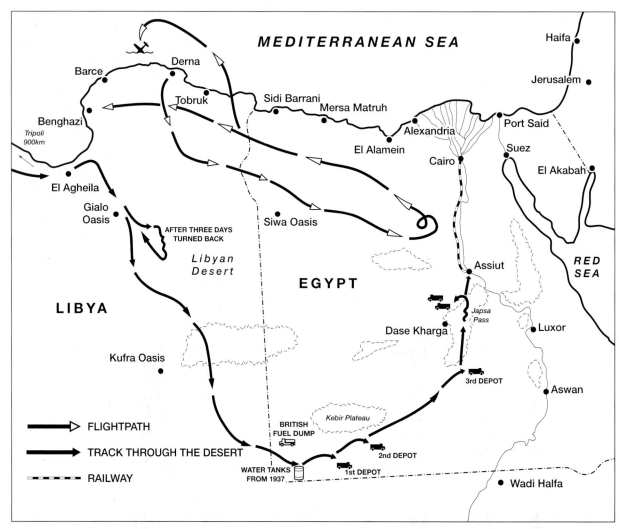

land and dodged Red Army patrols for several days. It reach the target area on the morning of the 9th and then reconnoitred the three bridges earmarked for destruction. The attack went in late on the 13th and, although sentries prevented one bridge from being destroyed, the other two were brought crashing down by explosive charges. Hettinger now retraced his steps, pursued all the way by Red Army units sent out to hunt this company down. Despite several firefights, the Brandenburgers reached Kairala late on the 16th.

THE BRANDENBURGERS IN NORTH AFRICA

Abwehr operatives had been in North Africa since from 1940 but the first large detachments appeared during June 1941 and the commitment escalated over the following months with the arrival of the Tropical Company under Lt Friedrich von Koenen. Gen Erwin Rommel was not immediately convinced of the Brandenburgers' value, but in September finally agreed to give them a free hand in intelligence-gathering, although he frowned on them wearing enemy uniforms. Brandenburgers had made two attempts to infiltrate Cairo to contact Arab nationalists who might be encouraged to openly rebel against the British. The missions, one codenamed 'Condor' in May and the second in July, both failed but in May 1942 the Brandenburgers successfully infiltrated two *Abwehr* agents into Egypt from Libya in an operation codenamed 'Salaam' (see box). However, for much of the year they conducted reconnaissance missions in the far south of the North African theatre in much the same way as Britain's SAS and Long-Range Desert Group.

A more ambitious mission under 2-Lt Helmut von Leipzig was devised in either June or July. Around 100 Brandenburgers, many fluent in a combination of Arabic, English or French, set out from Tripoli in a column of mostly captured vehicles and headed for Marzuq, an Italian garrison in southwest Libya, by way of Sabha. Their mission, codenamed 'Dora', was to conduct a long-range reconnaissance into Niger and Chad to assess the feasibility of severing the Allied supply lines that German intelligence believed ran across the interior between the Gulf of Guinea and Port Sudan. At Al-Qatrun, some 35 miles (56km) south of Marzuq, Leipzig established a forward base and split his detachment into three groups. One, under Leipzig himself, was despatched into neighbouring Algeria and struck out for the Tassili mountains in the country's far south on the border with Niger. The Brandenburgers were discovered by a French patrol and over the following days had to make a fighting retreat back across the border into Libya. The Brandenburgers escaped but four were killed by the French. The second group crossed over the Tibesti mountains in northern Chad and infiltrated the town of Bardai, only to discover that the company-strong garrison was soon to receive strong reinforcements. The decision was taken to return to Libya. 2-Lt von Leipzig's third group moved though Ghat in southwest Libya and crossed into southern Algeria, where it ran into a French-occupied village and was eventually forced to return to Algeria. The findings of 'Dora' suggested that the supply lines were only defended by comparatively small forces and could be cut by deploying a few divisions. However, Rommel had no divisions to spare and with the opening of the Battle of El Alamein in October and the 'Torch' landings in November he had more pressing matters to attend to. 'Dora' was quietly shelved.

By late 1942 the Axis forces in North Africa were in danger of being caught between two Allied forces advancing from west and east towards Tunisia. Brandenburgers were ordered to prevent British, French and US forces from reaching Tunisia before its defences could be arranged. In late October Koenen's Tropical Company left Libya for Tunisia, where it received reinforcements bringing it up to battalion strength. Their first operation, one involving 30 men, was against a bridge over the Wadi el-Kbir close to the village of Sidi Bou Baker in central Tunisia. The detachment left Bizerte airfield in three DFS 230

OPERATION 'SALAAM'

In spring 1942 the OKW ordered the *Abwehr* to infiltrate two men behind British lines in North Africa to gather intelligence that could be used by the newly arrived Afrika Korps under Gen Erwin Rommel in his drive on Egypt. A Brandenburger detachment in Libya was ordered to transport the two agents, Johannes Eppler and Gerd Sandstede, across the desert to their destination and then return to friendly lines, a round trip of some 4,000 miles (6,400km). The party was commanded by Capt Hans von Steffens, a fluent speaker of both English and Arabic, and he chose as his guide Hungarian-born Count Laszlo von Almásy, a veteran desert traveller. The plan was to use trucks to drive south down the Kufra track in east Cyrenaica to the oasis at Gialo and then motor east to reach the Yapsa Pass close to Asyut on the Nile River. From the pass the *Abwehr* agents would drive to Asiut and board a train for Cairo.

The operation began badly — within hours of setting out the trucks became stuck in soft sand and Steffens suffered a heart attack trying to dig them out. The party returned to base and made a second attempt without Steffens on 11 May. Almásy's desert experiences paid off and the team was able to reach the drop point without being discovered after 12 days even though they had to pass through checkpoints at the entrance to Yapsa. At the summit of the pass Almásy parted from the agents, who set off for Cairo, while he and his Brandenburgers retraced their steps, finally reaching safety at the beginning of June. The count radioed the completion of his mission to headquarters on the 4th but his labours proved worthless. The agents reached Cairo but British intelligence already knew of their plans and, once identified, the two men were tracked down to a houseboat on the Nile and arrested on October 14.

gliders late on 26 October. After landing, Koenen reconnoitred the bridge. The Brandenburgers then trekked over 120 miles (192km) to reach friendly lines at Maknassy six days later. A second team was less lucky; it successfully destroyed a bridge near Kasserine but was intercepted and its 10 men captured. Similar operations followed in early 1943. On 18 January a detachment led by 2-Lt Luchs destroyed a rail bridge carrying the Tozeur–Sfax line over the Wadi el-Melah in southern Tunisia. Like its predecessors, the mission was successful but could not prevent the inevitable defeat of the Axis forces in North Africa. However, most of the Brandenburgers did manage to escape to Sicily by boat before the German and Italian forces surrendered in the second week of May.

THE RISE OF OTTO SKORZENY

While the Brandenburgers continued to fight on the Eastern Front and elsewhere during 1942 and 1943, the battle between the *Abwehr* and SS security service continued. A further twist in the struggle took place on 27 May 1942. Heydrich, now Reich Protector of Bohemia, was assassinated in Prague by a group of Czech agents trained in Britain. The loss of the head of the RSHA would seem to benefit the *Abwehr* in its power struggle but Himmler took charge of its operations for the next several months and filled it with SS officers, who — like himself — were dedicated to rooting out anti-Nazi plots and destroying Canaris's intelligence machine. Chief among these was Walter Schellenberg, who was a senior figure in the RSHA's foreign secret service, and Ernst Kaltenbrunner, who eventually took over the running of the various SS security services from Himmler. As these men conspired, it became increasingly clear to them that the SS should establish a special force that could rival the exploits of the Brandenburgers and step into the breach once the *Abwehr* had been discredited. In 1942 Section VI of the RSHA, which was headed by Schellenberg at the time and responsible for intelligence-gathering, began organising a force similar to the Brandenburgers but filled with members of the Waffen-SS. In April 1943, a Waffen-SS officer, Capt Otto Skorzeny, was appointed to knock the unit into shape. The new units were known as *Friedenthaler Jagdverbände* (Friedenthal Hunting Groups) after the estate outside Berlin where they were based. These units placed special emphasis on anti-partisan operations and, like the Brandenburgers, sometimes wore foreign military uniforms or civilian clothes. However, Skorzeny had little time to complete the extensive training programme he had in mind as within a few months Hitler selected him to lead a daring mission to rescue Italian dictator Benito Mussolini

Mussolini had been removed from office on 23 July 1943 in a palace coup, led by King Victor Emmanuel III, the army's high command and assorted Fascist politicians. His prestige and authority had collapsed following the Allied victory in the North African campaign in May and the subsequent invasion of Sicily, Operation 'Husky', which had opened on 10 July. By this stage of the war it had became unquestionably clear that Italy had to surrender but that it was unlikely to secure favourable terms from the Allies with

Above: Another *Signal* image, the caption for this portrait of Reinhard Heydrich, SS-Obergruppenführer and General of Police, Reich Protector of of Bohemia and Moravia and a strong candidate for supreme office in the future, extolled the 'chivalrous fighter as statesman, as air pilot on the eastern and western fronts and as . . . one of the best European fencers.' On 27 May 1942, Heydrich was shot by British-trained Czech resistance fighters Josef Gabcik and Jan Kubis and died on 6 June of septicaemia. As a reprisal, the SS chose a village — Lidice — and killed all male inhabitants over the age of 16 years. Meanwhile, 1,331 Czechs, among them more than 200 women, were executed in Prague.

Mussolini still in power. After his arrest he was placed under close guard and over the following weeks was moved around at regular intervals by his captors, spending time at Frascati, Gaeta and the islands of Ponza and La Maddelena, before returning to mainland Italy. Hitler, who had greatly admired Mussolini in the latter's early years of power, could not let an old ally languish in captivity or possibly fall into Allied hands, and ordered that a rescue mission be undertaken. He placed the planning of the operation in the hands of the head of the Luftwaffe's paratroopers, Gen Kurt Student. The success of the mission depended on finding Mussolini and both Canaris's *Abwehr* and the RSHA's Schellenberg were ordered to find him.

The operation to rescue Mussolini was of the type that was ideally suited to the Brandenburgers, yet Hitler looked elsewhere for the men to attempt the top-secret mission and the officer to lead them into action. On 26 July he interviewed six officers from different branches of the armed forces at Rastenburg and after a brief conversion with each, selected Otto Skorzeny, like Hitler an Austrian by birth. Skorzeny flew to Italy the next day accompanied by 20 Luftwaffe paratroopers and landed at Practica di Mare airfield southeast of Rome on the coast, where around around 50 of his own troops were awaiting his arrival. Among these were Skorzeny's adjutant, SS Lt Karl Radl, a former member of the Brandenburgers. After a few false leads in August, one of which led Skorzeny to Maddalena on 26 August one hour after Mussolini had been moved by his captors, he was finally able to locate Mussolini definitively in early September thanks to his own intelligence officers and local informers. He discovered that the Italian dictator was being held on at the Albergo Rifugio, a hotel on one of the high ridges in the Gran Sasso massif approximately 60 miles (100km) northeast of Rome.

Skorzeny set to devising a plan and quickly ruled out a direct ground assault on the hotel, which could only be reached from the surrounding valley by a slow-moving funicular railway. Surprise and speed were the keys to success and he saw from high-altitude reconnaissance photographs taken from a Heinkel He111 on 8 September that a patch of seemingly flat ground close to the hotel was just large enough to land glider-borne troops. Skorzeny split his command, now with a strength of 108 men, into three parties: Skorzeny's, which was to be carried in 12 gliders, was tasked with landing by the hotel to rescue Mussolini; a battalion under Maj Mors was to secure the funicular railway station at the foot of the valley to prevent Italian troops from interfering in the rescue; a third was ordered to rescue Mussolini's wife and family who were being held at Rocca della Cominata.

Skorzeny ordered the operation to begin at 0600 hours on the 12th but the 12 DFS 230 gliders being transported to Practica del Mare from the French Riviera did not arrive until 1100 and a further delay was caused when an Allied air attack at around 1230 came close, but just failed, to destroy any of the aircraft. At 1300 hours the bulk of the armada took off for the one-hour flight to Gran Sasso except for two gliders that ran into bomb craters on the runway during take-off. The remaining gliders and their tugs climbed though clear skies, formed up and then set off for their destination. After a short

Above: Hitler had a great fellow-feeling for Mussolini, whose introduction of fascism in Italy had in many ways guided his own. The Blackshirts had gained power in 1922 — a year before the Munich Beer Hall Putsch. Thus Mussolini had been 'Il Duce' (leader) for more than ten years by 1933 when Hitler became the Führer (leader). He had already militarised Italy and engaged in expansionist policies — in 1935 he invaded Ethiopia and used poison gas to defeat the tribesmen. Initially Mussolini was unsure of Hitler but as the Nazi star began to rise, he supported the Nazis. He paid the price in July 1943, when he was arrested and imprisoned — leading to Skorzeny's mission to free him. Once freed, Hitler set up Mussolini as the leader of the Italian Socialist Republic in German-held northern Italy, and he would remain a German cipher until Axis forces surrendered in northern Italy in April 1945. Mussolini was arrested again and he and his mistress, Clara Petacci, were taken from the jail at Giulino di Messegra and lynched by the local Communist partisans. This photo is from the pages of *Signal*, where he was described as a statesman 'with the sure hand of a genius.'

Scenes from Skorzeny's daring rescue of Mussolini from the Hotel Albergo Rifugio high up in the Gran Sasso mountains on 12 September 1943. (See also colour pages 78–9.) For an excellent commentary on this rescue, many photographs taken at the time and postwar *After the Battle* issue 22 is essential reading. *All photos Bundesarchiv*

Opposite, above: A DFS 230 glider, possibly the one that Skorzeny used.

Opposite, below: From left to right — Skorzeny, dressed in a tropical Luftwaffe uniform (as were all those who took part in the operation), Mussolini and Inspector of Police Guiseppe Gueli.

Left: Rear view of the Hotel Albergo Rifugio.

Below and Below left: The rescue of Mussolini was re-enacted for the propaganda cameras by German Fallschirmjäger (Skorzeny and his team having left the area); these photographs are from the reconstruction.

time one of the tug pilots reported that he had lost contact with the two lead gliders in thick cloud and that they were nowhere to be seen, but Skorzeny ordered the mission to continue. Shortly before 1400, the planned assault time, Gran Sasso was spotted and Skorzeny ordered his pilot, Lt Meyer, to land the glider on the small patch of supposedly flat land close to the hotel, which on closer inspection turned out to be rocky and severely uneven. Nevertheless Meyer swooped toward the hotel, deployed the parachute break and made a crash-landing virtually on schedule.

Despite the danger of the rocks and boulders of the plateau, Skorzeny's glider, the first to land, skidded to a halt no more than 16.5 yards (15m) from the hotel. He led his men forward, ordering that none was to fire unless he gave the order. A lone Carabinieri sentry on guard at one corner of the hotel surrendered immediately, and the assault group led by its commander ran through an open door. A second guard, this time seated at a wireless set, was spotted and Skorzeny kicked the chair from under him and smashed the set with his machine-pistol. The band then returned outside, moved round the walls of the building and then, again with Skorzeny in the lead, scaled a 10ft (3m) terrace. Mussolini's face suddenly appeared at a first-floor window and was hurriedly waved away by Skorzeny. Brushing aside a number of Italian sentries who were quickly overpowered, Skorzeny charged into a large hallway and up a broad staircase on the right. Racing to the top he flung open the first doorway and was greeted by the sight of the dictator and two officers. These two guards were bundled aside — Mussolini had been rescued in under five minutes and no shots had been fired by either side.

While Skorzeny was rescuing Mussolini, the other gliders had come in to land but one was caught by a strong gust of wind, crashed out of control and was smashed on the rocks. The reinforcements that did land faced a brief firefight with the few Carabinieri that had not surrendered but these gave up when the Italian colonel of the garrison agreed to hang a white surrender flag from one of the hotel's windows. Skorzeny also heard that Mors's detachment had successfully captured the funicular railway station at the foot of the valley and ordered him to bring his men up to the Albergo Rifugio. Skorzeny now selected one of three pre-planned means of speedily moving Mussolini to safety. Two had already effectively failed: a surprise assault on the Aquila de Abruzzi airfield at the foot of the valley at 1600 followed by the landing of transport He111s was rejected as Skorzeny could not contact the assault group, and the plan to use a small Fieseler Storch landing close to the funicular station ended when the aircraft was badly damaged on landing. The third plan was to land a similar aircraft directly on to the plateau, a risky proposition. The pilot, Lt Gerlach,

Below: Man hanged by German anti-partisan forces in Yugoslavia, Belgrade autumn 1941. The soldiers are possibly Brandenburgers who were known to be there at the time. *via Chris Ellis*

nevertheless made a successful landing and he, Skorzeny and Mussolini took off in what was a grossly overloaded aircraft. After landing at Practica di Mare, Mussolini and Skorzeny transferred to an He111 and immediately flew to an airfield at Aspern on the outskirts of Vienna, where it was confirmed that Mussolini's family had arrived in Munich after an equally successful rescue from Rocca della Caminata. After accompanying Mussolini to Rastenburg, Skorzeny returned to Italy, where he discovered that the Gran Sasso operation was to be turned into a propaganda event.

THE FALL OF THE *ABWEHR* AND THE BRANDENBURGERS

The joint Luftwaffe–SS operation rescue was a brilliant success but, much to Student's annoyance, it was Skorzeny and his men, not the Luftwaffe, that received the accolades. Skorzeny was awarded the Knight's Cross and promoted to SS-Sturmbannführer (major) by Hitler, who recognised the enormous propaganda value of the successful rescue at a time when the German people were increasingly starved of good news from the fighting fronts. Gran Sasso also marked a decisive moment in the *Abwehr*'s — and Brandenburgers' — fall from grace and the rise of the SS and its intelligence agencies to a position of unchallenged power. Hitler had already been made aware of the *Abwehr*'s likely involvement in anti-Nazi plots, not least Operation 'U-7', by both Himmler and his senior deputies, including Schellenberg, head of the SD. 'U-7' was masterminded by Canaris's deputy, Hans Oster, and involved smuggling Jewish refugees from Germany to Switzerland. It was finally uncovered in February 1943 and Oster was subsequently dismissed from his post. Coming on top of this, the *Abwehr*'s failure to find Mussolini, deliberate or otherwise, further convinced Hitler that the organisation was at the very least unreliable if not outright treacherous from top to bottom. The *Abwehr* continued to function for several more months but both it and Canaris were completely marginalised by the SS. It was finally broken up in February 1944. Canaris was briefly ordered to keep away from Berlin and all intelligence operations were placed under the control of Himmler's SS.

Above: Lt-Gen Karl Student, Luftwaffe commander of XI Flieger Corps and nominally in charge of Mussolini's rescue. *via Chris Ellis*

The collapse of the *Abwehr* signalled the demise of the Brandenburgers as they were originally constituted. From late 1942 the unit became involved in anti-partisan activities and conventional combat roles on the Eastern Front and in the Balkans, neither of which reflected the value of its men's training or experience. Losses were high and morale undoubtedly suffered. The *Abwehr*, which was under intense pressure from the SS, also began to lose interest in the unit and it came increasingly under the direct control of the OKW. An OKW order retitled the three regiments *Sonderverbände* (Special Units) Nos 801, 802 and 803 in January 1943, and a fourth special unit, *Sonderverband* No 804, was added to the order of battle. These battalions acted as the cadre for the four regiments that would make up the Brandenburg Division from April. It was commanded by Maj-Gen Alexander von Pfuhlstein and contained the four *Sonderverbände* plus various other detachments including four tropical

Below: Hostages shot at Chabatz by anti-partisan forces (possibly Brandenburgers) in Yugoslavia as retribution for attack by Mikailovich's Chetniks, autumn 1941. *via Chris Ellis*

companies and a parachute battalion. There was also the *Küstenjäger Abteilung* (Coastal Raider Detachment) made up of volunteers from the Kriegsmarine. Little is known of its missions but its motorboats were initially based on the Dalmatian coast and subsequently took part in Operation '*Eisbär*', (polar bear) the occupation of the Dodecanese island of Cos (see map below), in October 1943 and the capture of Leros a month later (see pages 38–9). The division never fought as a single entity during 1943–4 as detachments were used where and when they were needed.

Although Brandenburger detachments conducted special operations with some noteworthy successes, particularly the occupation of Leros, the rapid expansion severely undermined their capabilities. New recruits were not of the same calibre as the first; out of 14,000 men in the division in mid-1944, for example, only 900 spoke a foreign language. To make matters worse Pfuhlstein was implicated in the anti-Nazi *Schwarze Kapelle* resistance movement that was being hunted by the Gestapo and was dismissed in April 1944 — seemingly further confirmation of the *Abwehr*'s unreliability. Pfuhlstein's dismissal, which closely followed the destruction of the *Abwehr* the previous February, ensured the Brandenburg Division would lose its role to the SS, chiefly the various forces that operated under Hitler's new favourite, Otto Skorzeny.

The Brandenburgers, now commanded by Lt-Gen Kühlwein, conducted a few special operations in the months after Pfuhlstein's dismissal. Its 1st Regiment played a supporting role in Operation '*Rösselsprung*' (knight's move), an attack on Marshal Tito's headquarters near Drvar in Yugoslavia in May (see pages 42–4 below), when it was ordered to push from Knin toward Grahovo and then move on Drvar as part of a move to cut off the partisans' line of retreat.

Below: The German attack on Cos. Defended by 1st Battalion, the Durham Light Infantry, two squadrons of RAF Regiment and the Italian garrison, Cos was a hard nut to crack. The German invading force comprised 22nd Infantry Division and two companies of Brandenburgers — 1st Küstenjäger (KJA), equivalent to the British SBS or US Navy SEALs, and a parachute company. The landings took place on 3 October 1943 and by the end of the next day the Germans were in control of the island; Lt-Col L. R. F. Kenyon, CO of the Durhams, had been taken prisoner as had nearly 1,400 British troops for the cost of 14 German dead.

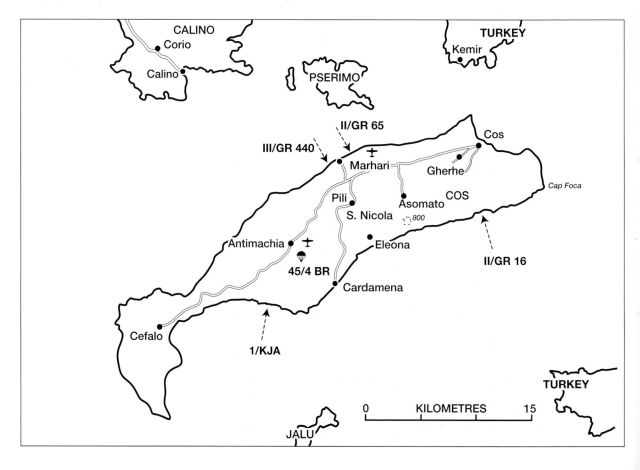

The Brandenburgers were again in action in the Balkans during the following August. The Red Army was close to Romania's borders and the country's figurehead sovereign, King Michael I, pushed forward armistice negotiations with the Soviet Union. Both he and some of his generals also suspected the pro-Nazi head of government, Prime Minister Ion Antonescu, would do little to prevent a full-blown German occupation in the event of Romania's defection from the Axis

Above: German forces landing on Cos. The German actions in the Dodecanese were the last significant use of the Brandenburgers who performed with distinction. Unfortunately, the aftermath of the invasions was the execution of most of the Italian personnel on the islands — over 100 officers were slaughtered on Cos; nearly 5,000 Italian soldiers had been systematically executed on Cephalonia in late September. The German commander, was executed on 20 May 1947 in Athens for these crimes. *via Chris Ellis*

alliance. On the night of the 23rd Michael staged a coup, arresting Antonescu and his cabinet, and ordered his forces to change sides. Hitler feared the collapse of the southern sector of the Eastern Front and ordered an attack on Bucharest. Part of the Brandenburg Division's 3rd Regiment, some two company and support elements, along with its parachute battalion were ordered to the capital. Their role was twofold: to occupy Otopeni airport and rescue two generals and their staffs who had been surrounded by their former Romanian allies at their command post, Waldlager I, near the airfield.

The first Brandenburgers arrived by air at midday on the 24th and quickly began securing Otopeni. Over the following hours more Brandenburgers were flown into Bucharest in huge Messerschmitt Me323 Gigants and by about 2000 hours Waldlager I had been reached. After some tense negotiations, the generals and staffs, along with a Brandenburger escort, were given permission to head for the Yugoslavian border. However, the Romanians reneged on the deal and the generals, their staff and the majority of the Brandenburgers were surrounded and forced to surrender. Most were handed over to the advancing Red Army.

Despite these commando-style operations the transformation of the division continued. It was officially retitled the Panzergrenadier Division Brandenburg on 8 September but some 350 Brandenburgers objected to the new role and joined Skorzeny's units. After a period of reorganisation the new division's scattered units were assembled at the Mauerwald camp, East Prussia, in mid-December and henceforth served as a wholly conventional force, mostly on the Eastern Front. In the latter stages of the conflict it fought as part of the Grossdeutschland Panzer Corps, which also included the Grossdeutschland Panzergrenadier Division and the Luftwaffe's Hermann Göring Panzer Division.

The Panzergrenadier Division Brandenburg under Maj-Gen Hermann Schulte-Heuthaus joined the newly formed corps on 12 January 1945, and was immediately flung into action around Lodz in Poland. It was forced to retreat westward by the pincer attacks of the Red Army until by the end of the month it was holding positions along the Neisse River north of Görlitz. Between late February and mid-April the division fought bitter battles on the Neisse between Muskau and Steinback but was eventually forced to retreat in Czechoslovakia, where its men surrendered or escaped westward in the final days of the war.

OPERATION 'LEOPARD'/'TYPHOON' — THE CAPTURE OF LEROS

Italy's surrender in September 1943 left a power vacuum on the Dodecanese islands in the Aegean Sea that both Britain and Germany attempted to fill. The British hastily gathered together a small force and by early October had control of eight Dodecanese islands and Samos to the north of the group. One of their key positions was Leros, a seaplane base protected by several coastal batteries defended by around 9,000 British and pro-Allied Italian troops by early November.

Although the British had moved quickly, German troops still held the large islands of Crete and Rhodes, as well as mainland Greece, and Hitler, who feared that the Dodecanese would be used as bases for landings in the Balkans, ordered the lost islands retaken. Although the Germans had few ground troops for the operation, they did enjoy air superiority and the British, heavily committed on the Italian mainland, had few reserves available to bolster their garrisons.

Cos was the first German target and it fell easily after landings, on 3 October that involved the 1st Company of the Brandenburg Division's *Küstenjäger Abteilung*. Leros was targeted in mid-November and the Brandenburg Division provided the same coastal company as fought on Cos as well as part of its 4th Regiment's 15th Parachute Company and detachments from the 1st Regiment's IIIrd Battalion for the invasion, which was initially codenamed 'Leopard' (this was

changed to *'Taifun'* — Typhoon — on 2 November). The operation opened on 12 November after major attacks by the Luftwaffe on the various batteries. The guns were not destroyed. The parachute company plus similar Luftwaffe units were recalled after running into intense antiaircraft fire over their landing zone, while an invasion flotilla heading for Gurna Bay was also beaten back by fire from coastal batteries. Initially only the eastern task force was able to secure two small footholds at Alinda Day close to Leros town. The paratroopers tried again and this time secured a defensive perimeter on Rachi ridge between the two bays. In the east the Brandenburgers were also able to land at Pandeli Bay to the south of Leros town and after a hard climb gain a foothold on Mount Appetici that they were temporarily unable to exploit.

The battle was stalemated but on the 13th German reinforcements reached the island to prevent the British destroying the scattered bridgeheads before they could be expanded. On the 14th and 15th Brandenburgers beat off several British counterattacks and the following day the 1st Regiment's IIIrd Battalion arrived. Going straight into action they captured Mount Meraviglia, site of the British headquarters to the south of Leros town, on the 17th and organised resistance collapsed.

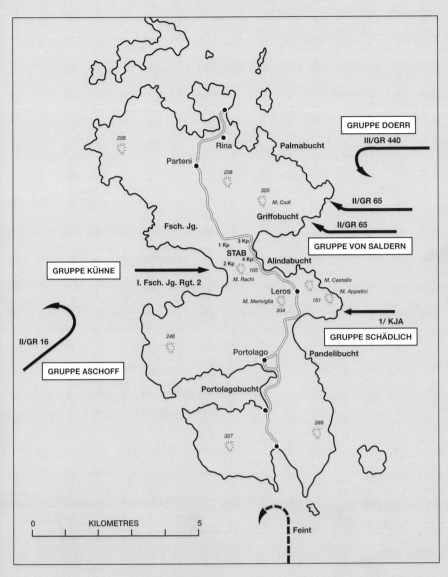

GRUPPE DOERR
III/GR 440

II/GR 65

II/GR 65

GRUPPE VON SALDERN

GRUPPE KÜHNE
I. Fsch. Jg. Rgt. 2

GRUPPE SCHÄDLICH
1/ KJA

II/GR 16

GRUPPE ASCHOFF

256

238

320
M. Cudi

Rina
Parteni
Palmabucht

Fsch. Jg.

Griffobucht

3 Kp
1 Kp
STAB
4 Kp
2 Kp
105
M. Rachi
Alindabucht

M. Castello
M. Appetici
Leros
M. Meriviglia
181
204

248

Portolago
Pandelibucht

Portolagobucht

327

288

0   KILOMETRES   5

Feint

Far left: Bombs exploding near village of Portolago on Leros during the German invasion of 12 November 1943. *via Chris Ellis*

Left: The five invading groups. The Brandenburg Küstenjäger (KJA) were under the command of Lt Hans Schädlich.

Below left: British and Italian prisoners after capture on Leros (they totalled 8,850). *via Chris Ellis*

Below: Brig RAG Tilney (right) commander of the British garrison after the capture of Leros, being interviewed by German commander Gen Friedrich-Wilhelm Müller (left), CG of 22nd Infantry Division, on 16 November 1943. Müller was executed on 20 May 1947 in Athens for war crimes. *via Chris Ellis*

BRANDENBURG-LEHR-REGIMENT zbV 800 MAY 1940–DECEMBER 1942

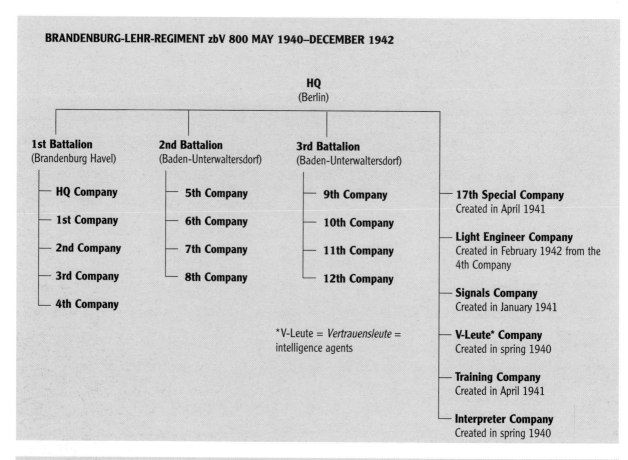

HQ
(Berlin)

1st Battalion
(Brandenburg Havel)

- HQ Company
- 1st Company
- 2nd Company
- 3rd Company
- 4th Company

2nd Battalion
(Baden-Unterwaltersdorf)

- 5th Company
- 6th Company
- 7th Company
- 8th Company

3rd Battalion
(Baden-Unterwaltersdorf)

- 9th Company
- 10th Company
- 11th Company
- 12th Company

- **17th Special Company**
  Created in April 1941
- **Light Engineer Company**
  Created in February 1942 from the
  4th Company
- **Signals Company**
  Created in January 1941
- **V-Leute* Company**
  Created in spring 1940
- **Training Company**
  Created in April 1941
- **Interpreter Company**
  Created in spring 1940

*V-Leute = *Vertrauensleute* =
intelligence agents

BRANDENBURG DIVISION APRIL 1943–SEPTEMBER 1943

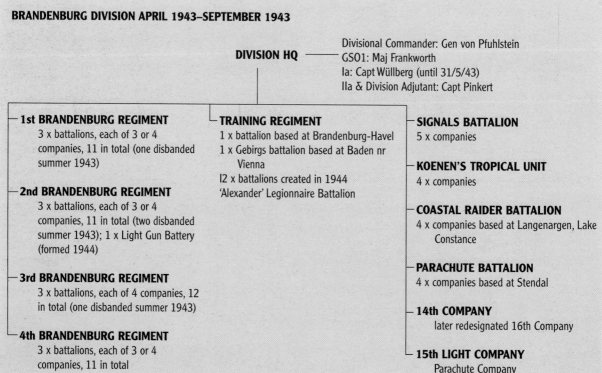

DIVISION HQ —
Divisional Commander: Gen von Pfuhlstein
GSO1: Maj Frankworth
Ia: Capt Wüllberg (until 31/5/43)
IIa & Division Adjutant: Capt Pinkert

1st BRANDENBURG REGIMENT
3 x battalions, each of 3 or 4
companies, 11 in total (one disbanded
summer 1943)

2nd BRANDENBURG REGIMENT
3 x battalions, each of 3 or 4
companies, 11 in total (two disbanded
summer 1943); 1 x Light Gun Battery
(formed 1944)

3rd BRANDENBURG REGIMENT
3 x battalions, each of 4 companies, 12
in total (one disbanded summer 1943)

4th BRANDENBURG REGIMENT
3 x battalions, each of 3 or 4
companies, 11 in total

TRAINING REGIMENT
1 x battalion based at Brandenburg-Havel
1 x Gebirgs battalion based at Baden nr
  Vienna
I2 x battalions created in 1944
'Alexander' Legionnaire Battalion

SIGNALS BATTALION
5 x companies

KOENEN'S TROPICAL UNIT
4 x companies

COASTAL RAIDER BATTALION
4 x companies based at Langenargen, Lake
  Constance

PARACHUTE BATTALION
4 x companies based at Stendal

14th COMPANY
  later redesignated 16th Company

15th LIGHT COMPANY
  Parachute Company

PANZERGRENADIER-DIVISION BRANDENBURG FROM SEPTEMBER 1943

Division HQ
- HQ & HQ Company
  - Machine Gun Platoon
  - Motorcycle Platoon
  - Flak Platoon (self-propelled)
  - Mortar Platoon
- Mapping Detachment (mot)
- Military Police Detachment (mot)

1st Jäger Regiment
HQ & HQ Company
- HQ Platoon
- Signals Platoon
- Motorcycle Platoon

- Panzergrenadier Battalion (half-track)
  - HQ
  - Supply Company (mot)
  - 3 x Company (half-track)
  - Heavy Company
    - Staff Platoon
    - Mortar Platoon
    - Light Infantry Gun Platoon

- Jäger Battalion (mot)
  - HQ
  - Supply Company
  - 3 x Company (mot)
  - 2 x Heavy Company (mot)

- Heavy Infantry Gun Company (SP)

- Pioneer Company (mot)
  - HQ (half-track)
  - 4 x Platoon (half-track)

2nd Jäger Regiment
- HQ & HQ Company
  - Staff Platoon
  - Signals Platoon
  - Motorcycle Platoon

- 2 x Jäger Battalion (mot)
  - HQ
  - Supply Company
  - 3 x Company (mot)
  - 2 x Heavy Company (mot)

- Heavy Infantry Gun Company (SP)

- Pioneer Company (mot)

Artillery Regiment
HQ & HQ Company
- Battalion
  - HQ & HQ Battery (SP)
  - Flak Battalion (SP)
  - 2 x Light Howitzer Battery (SP)
  - heavy Howitzer Battery (SP)
- Battalion
  - HQ & HQ Company (mot)
  - Flak Platoon (mot)
  - 3 x Light Battery (mot)
- Battalion
  - HQ & HQ Company (mot)
  - Flak Platoon (mot)
  - 3 x Heavy Battery (mot)

Pioneer Battalion
- HQ & HQ Company
- 2 x Company (mot)
- Company (self-propelled)

Panzerjäger Battalion
- HQ & HQ Battery
- Sturmgeschütz Staff Platoon
- 2 x Sturmgeschütz Company
- Panzerjäger Company (mot)
- Panzerjäger Supply Company (mot)

Signals Battalion
- HQ
- Telephone Company
- Radio Company
- Signals Supply Column (mot)

Panzer Regiment
HQ & HQ Company
- Signals Platoon
- Pioneer Platoon
- Flak Platoon (SP)
- Panzer Maintenance Company
- 2 x Battalion
  - HQ & HQ Company
  - 4 x Panzer Company
  - Flak Company (SP)
  - Supply Company (mot)

Reconnaissance Battalion
- HQ
  - Armoured Car Platoon
  - Signals Platoon (mot)
- Armoured Car Company (half-track)
- 3 x Reconnaissance Company (half-track)
- Reconnaissance Supply Company

Army Flak Battalion
HQ & HQ Battery
- 2 x Battery (mot)
- Light Flak Battery
- Flak Section (self-propelled)
- Searchlight Section

Supply & Support Units

As the Brandenburgers' fortunes declined in the second half of the war, Skorzeny's stock continued to rise. In late 1943, after the rescue of Mussolini, he was ordered to oversee a large expansion of the SS's special forces that were effectively to replace the Brandenburgers. He was authorised to raise No 502 Special Services Battalion and took recruits from every branch of the armed forces, including the Brandenburg Division. Indeed, Baron Adrian von Foelkersam led a deputation of 11 Brandenburger officers that were eventually permitted to join Skorzeny's troops by a reluctant Canaris in November after months of fractious argument. He also had the 500th SS Parachute Battalion placed under his direction and took on even more wide-ranging roles. Skorzeny was involved in the development and deployment of specialist naval forces, chiefly midget submarines and frogmen, and worked closely with Kampfgruppe 200, the Luftwaffe's special operations unit, on developing a piloted version of the V1 rocket. Various schemes were hatched involving Skorzeny's forces. These included sabotage raids against oil pipelines in the Middle East, a scheme to use frogmen to block the Suez Canal and an attack on the Russian oilfields around Baku on the shores of the Caspian Sea. None of these raids reached fruition, partly because by the beginning of 1944 Germany was facing more immediate threats, especially on the Eastern Front and in the Balkans.

OPERATION '*RÖSSELSPRUNG*' — THE ATTACK ON TITO'S HEADQUARTERS

By this stage of the war the Yugoslav partisan leader Tito had command of a force numbering perhaps 250,000 men and women and controlled to some degree probably a third of Yugoslavia, mostly its mountainous rural areas. German forces had made frequent attempts to destroy the partisans beginning in September 1941 and, although they had scored some significant successes against Tito's originally weak forces, by early 1944 it was apparent that a further blow had to be stuck against the partisans before they could gather strength from supplies provided by the western Allies, chiefly Britain, and the ongoing collapse of the pro-German Ustasa government in the puppet Independent State of Croatia. Germany lacked the resources to launch a major offensive against the partisans because of growing crises elsewhere, so plans were laid to launch a surgical strike against Tito's headquarter's complex, which lay at Drvar in western Bosnia, either to kill or to capture the partisan leader. Skorzeny was dubious about the operation's chances of success for two reasons: because of its complexity and because he feared that the partisans had got wind of the plan. (He feared this with justification: they had!) Nevertheless, his SS 500th Parachute Battalion, was ordered to take part in the operation, which was codenamed *Rösselsprung* (knight's move). The plan called for ground units to approach Tito's sprawling headquarters complex from various directions while the parachute battalion dropped on the camp killed or captured Tito and then fought off the partisans until relieved.

Intelligence about Tito's precise whereabouts came from Brandenburgers, who had been operating clandestinely among the local population since before the fifth major sweep against the partisans, which opened in May 1943 and dragged on through the following summer. Shortly before the beginning of *Rösselsprung* in May 1944, they discovered that he was based in a cave at Bastasi some three miles (5km) from Drvar, and a deserter later indicated that he was guarded by around 350 partisans. It soon became apparent to Skorzeny, who had recently arrived in Yugoslavia, that *Rösselsprung* was common knowledge among local civilians and, therefore, also among the partisans. Despite this security lapse, preparations for the raid continued. The parachute battalion's commander, SS Lt Rybka, was forced to abandon the plan for a single landing because

Below: Hitler and Skorzeny.

Left: Ion Antonescu (1882–1946), Romanian marshal and dictator, served in World War I and in early September 1940 became premier of Romania. Completely pro-Nazi he forced King Carol to abdicate in favour of Carol's son, Michael, and two months later joined the Axis powers. Antonescu gave Hitler virtual control over the Romanian economy and foreign policy, allowed anti-Semitic pogroms and joined in the war against Russia on 22 June 1941. In August 1944 King Michael had Antonescu and his cabinet arrested and joined the Allied side. Antonescu was executed for war crimes in 1946. Romania was important to the Nazis because of its oil supplies, particularly around Ploesti, and because a number of Romanian divisions were fighting alongside the German forces. In an attempt to retrieve the situation the Brandenburgers were sent in to Bucharest. *TRH Pictures*

Below: The unit chosen for the Romanian mission (see page 39) was part of the 3rd Regiment. They were transported to Otopeni airport on 24 August in Messerschmitt Me323 Gigants (as here) — but the mission was to end badly for the Brandenburgers. After securing Antonescu and his staff they were surrounded by Romanian troops and forced to surrender.

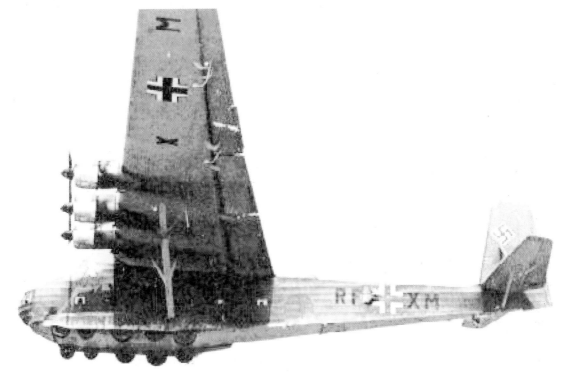

of shortages of gliders and transport aircraft. He was, therefore, forced to split his battalion: the first wave, some 320 men, was split into several detachments and each was allocated a specific target within the complex. The 100 men of Panther Group was tasked with the most important, that of seeking out Tito in his personal headquarters, known as the Citadel. The others were to destroy the various military missions from Britain, the Soviet Union and the United States that were attached to the headquarters or smash communication links with the various partisan bands operating in the area. The second wave was to help out where necessary.

The 55-minute flight to the target area began shortly after dawn on 25 May and the paratroopers began jumping over Drvar and the Citadel, the target areas, from the low-flying Junkers Ju52 transports shortly before 0700 hours. Twenty seconds later the first men were on the ground and secured a perimeter into which the troops aboard DFS 230 gliders could set down. In Drvar there was limited opposition and several groups secured their objectives with few casualties but at the Citadel itself Panther Group was pinned down by the partisans, taking heavy casualties from numerous well-sited defensive positions. Rybka ordered the rest of his command to aid Panther Group but it soon became apparent that his lightly equipped men were running low on ammunition while the partisans were rushing more and more units to the battlefield. By 0930 hours the paratroopers were no longer fighting to capture the Citadel but were battling to hold out until reinforcements could arrive. The second wave of paratroopers arrived but landed in an area swept by machine-gun and mortar fire. Losses were high but the survivors among the original 300 or so linked up with Rybka. Around midday, the paratroopers launched another attack against the Citadel but it ended in failure with their commander wounded.

The loss of Rybka confirmed the battalion's plight. It was virtually surrounded by a large — and getting larger — number of partisans, was increasingly desperate for resupply, and had seen no sight of the battlegroup from 373rd Division that was supposed to relieve it. In the late afternoon the order was given to fall back from the hill on which the Citadel lay and regroup in Drvar, particularly around the town's cemetery. Harassed by the partisans, the final paratroopers did not reach its foot until around 2200 hours and then headed for the town. Throughout the night the partisans launched several attacks against the cemetery, the last coming at dawn on the 26th. Daylight allowed the Luftwaffe to bomb and strafe the partisans, who gradually fell back, and saw the arrival of troops from the 13th Regiment of the 7th SS Mountain Division Prinz Eugen. The

Below: Brandenburger movements during Operation 'Rösselsprung', May 1944.

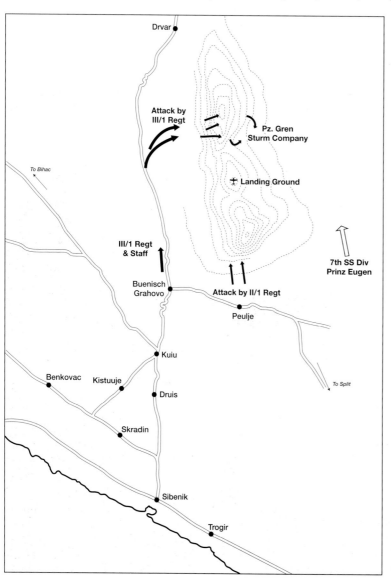

paratroopers' ordeal was finally over but it was clear that their mission had failed; Tito, although slightly wounded, had escaped the trap and the parachute battalion had been effectively destroyed as a fighting force. It would be reconstituted but was ultimately destroyed fighting the Red Army on the Eastern Front.

OPERATION 'PANZERFAUST' — SKORZENY IN HUNGARY

On 10 September 1944 Skorzeny attended various briefings at Rastenburg and in the evening attended an informal post-dinner conference with Hitler and a handful of of other leading Nazis. Talk drifted to discussion of the worsening situation along the whole length of the Eastern Front and the ongoing defection of Germany's eastern allies. The Soviet summer offensive had thrown the German forces out of western Russia and had reached the line of the Vistula River in Poland by August, while to the north Finland had agreed a truce with the Soviet Union on 4 September. In the Balkans, Romania was virtually overrun the Red Army; Bulgaria had defected from the Axis alliance on the 8th; Romania was about to fall to the Red Army after having capitulated on 23 August, and German troops in Greece and Yugoslavia were falling back to avoid encirclement in the southern Balkans. Hitler also suspected that Hungary was again looking for a way out of the war; he had already sent his troops into the country the previous March after intelligence reports had indicated that the Hungarian regent, Admiral Miklós Horthy, had contacted both the western Allies and the Soviet Union to discuss armistice terms. Although Horthy had been browbeaten by the German occupation, by September Soviet forces were arrayed on the east Hungarian border and the regent was again sending out peace feelers. Hitler, who feared the loss of Hungary's oilfields and grain supplies as well as the possible cutting off of 70 divisions fighting in the Balkans, correctly suspected that Horthy was again contemplating secret discussions with the Allies and ordered Skorzeny to prepare a mission to install a pliant puppet regime to ensure that Hungary would go on fighting.

Below: SS-Sturmbannführer Otto Skorzeny and SS-Obersturmführer Adrian von Foelkersam shown in Budapest in October 1944 after Operation 'Panzerfaust'. Bundesarchiv

What Hitler had suspected in that September discussion with Skorzeny was confirmed on 15 October, when Horthy made a radio broadcast to the Hungarian people announcing that a preliminary armistice had been agreed with the Soviet Union four days before. The takeover operation had been devised in the immediate aftermath of the Rastenburg meeting. Travelling incognito as a Doctor Wolf, Skorzeny arrived in Budapest on 12 September and quickly discovered that the chief Hungarian negotiator was the regent's own son, Niklas, and that he had regular meetings with Yugoslavian intermediaries selected by Marshal Tito. Skorzeny, who had infiltrated some of his own men into the capital, decided to aid the Gestapo by capturing Niklas Horthy the next time he met the Yugoslavians in Budapest. If Niklas Horthy were in German custody, Skorzeny reasoned, his father might break off the armistice negotiations. The plan, was codenamed 'Mickey Mouse' and, after one aborted attempt, finally took place on 15 October. Skorzeny's company waited in a side street close to the building where the meeting was to take place, while he parked his car in the square on which the target stood. Gestapo officers were already in the building, on the floor above the meeting room, and others were to enter from the square shortly

Above: Belgrade is liberated by the partisans on 20 October 1944 — the name derived from the *partidas*, Spanish guerrilla bands that had harassed Napoleon during his invasions of Spain and Russia. Their importance to the Allied cause cannot be overlooked. In 1943, at a time when two German divisions were defending Sicily against the combined might of Britain and the United States, seven German divisions were being mauled by Tito's partisans. It is unsurprising, therefore, that the Germans spent so much time trying to kill Tito. *TRH Pictures*

Right: The German retreat from Greece and the Balkans in 1944.

Left: Tito (1892–1980) was born Josip Broz, the son of a Croatian blacksmith. He fought in Russia with the Austro-Hungarian army in World War I and then served with distinction in the Red Army during the Russian civil war of 1918–20. A prominent union organiser, he was imprisoned as a political agitator 1929–34, but in 1941 he emerged as a leader of the Yugoslav resistance after the defeat and occupation of Yugoslavia by the Axis powers. In spite of the opposition of the Yugoslav government in exile, which supported the Serbian resistance leader Mikailovich and his Chetniks, adopting the name Tito, Josip Broz welded together a force primarily of communists, although there were many non-communists, bedfellows in part because of the appeal of Tito's dream of a federated Yugoslavia but also because of Tito's character. Unknown at first to the outside world (partly because of Mikailovich), in 1941, when Hitler's forces took the Balkans, the head of the outlawed Communist Party of Yugoslavia was a shadowy figure; there was so much confusion about his identity that some people thought the name Tito stood for a terrorist organisation. On the ground, however, there was no doubt about who Tito was. A brilliant guerrilla tactician and a forceful, charismatic personality, by 1943 Tito headed a large army and controlled a sizable part of Yugoslavia, centred in Bosnia. He fought alongside his men supported from the start by the Soviet Union, and from 1944 by Britain and the United States. In November 1944 he liberated Belgrade. In March 1945 he became head of the new federal Yugoslav government, going on to execute Mikailovich, depose King Peter II, proclaim a republic and rule dictatorially until his death.

The Germans tried many times to kill Tito (including the Brandenburgers' attempt by Operation '*Rösselsprung*'): 'He was always encircled,' remarked Heinrich Himmler, 'and the man found a way out every time.' *TRH Pictures*

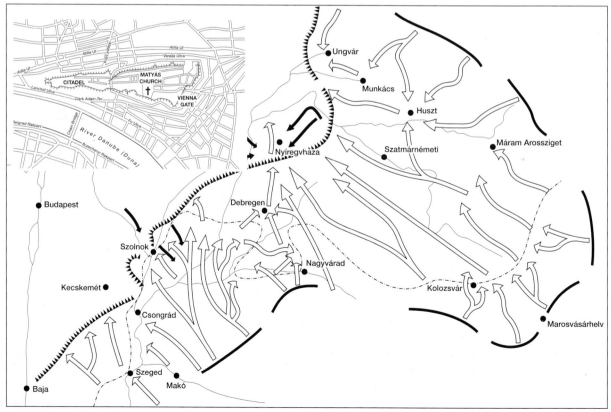

after 1000 hours to make the arrests. The first Gestapo man entered on schedule but the second aroused the suspicion of the Hungarian guards parked outside the entrance and was shot. Skorzeny immediately went into action, calling for his detachment in the side-street to join him as a vicious but brief firefight broke out with Hungarian troops hidden in buildings along the sides of the square. As this ended the Gestapo men and Skorzeny brought Horthy and a second Hungarian conspirator out of the building wrapped in large rugs to hide their identity and bundled them into a truck. The captives were taken to a convenient airfield and flown out of Hungary to spend the remainder of the war as 'guests' of the Germans.

'Mickey Mouse' had taken just ten minutes and over the next few hours Skorzeny waited anxiously for the regent's reaction. It came later that afternoon, at 1400 hours, when Horthy made the radio announcement that revealed the ongoing peace negotiations with the Soviet Union and that hostilities would cease with immediate effect. Clearly Operation 'Mickey Mouse' had not had the desired result but Skorzeny responded rapidly. He contacted the recently arrived commander of the nearby German troops, SS Gen Erich von dem Bach-Zelewski, and persuaded him to throw a cordon around the strongly defended Castle Hill, the regent's official residence and location of many other government buildings. Bach-Zelewski, who had recently razed Warsaw to the ground, suggested that similar action against Budapest would bring the Hungarians to heel, but Skorzeny wanted a subtler approach. The general's troops were to surround Castle Hill and make obvious but leisurely moves to lay siege to the government complex. While the Hungarians were occupied by this ruse, he would launch a surgical strike to apprehend the regent with a small detachment. The operation was codenamed 'Panzerfaust' after the German single-shot disposable anti-tank rocket-launcher.

Skorzeny's main assault team, a mixture of Waffen-SS paratroopers and his own Mitte battalion, was supported by four Panther tanks and a number of Goliaths — remote-controlled tracked explosive devices that were to be used to clear any barricades (see pages 74–5).

At dawn the next day, Skorzeny's detachment formed up close to Castle Hill and then followed the winding road to the complex's Vienna Gate. The attack was supported by a battalion of naval cadets from the Wiener-Neustadt Kriegsakademie, which advanced though garden's on the citadel's southern slope, a platoon of Skorzeny's own Mitte battalion moved on the western side supported by a pair of Panthers, while a platoon of the 600th SS Parachute Battalion advanced through a tunnel to reach the Hungarian Ministries of War and Home Affairs. A Luftwaffe paratrooper battalion acted as a reserve. Skorzeny feared that mines might delay his progress but this proved unfounded as the Hungarians had removed them in an attempt to defuse the tense situation but the detachment reached the citadel without arousing undue suspicion and, crashing through a barricade, entered its central square. As a firefight developed, Skorzeny made his way to the commandant's office and demanded that he surrender the citadel immediately. Ten minutes later the sounds of battle died away, leaving German forces in charge of all of the main government buildings. Skorzeny discovered that the regent was already in the custody of SS Lt-Gen Karl Pfeffer-Wildenbruch. 'Panzerfaust' was a brilliant coup and cost the lives of just four German troops, with a further 12 men wounded. Hungarian casualties were equally low, just four dead and 12 wounded. The regent's abdication was swiftly announced and Skorzeny later accompanied him on the train journey that took him into German captivity. A new government under a pro-German prime minister, Count Szalasi, was formed. One of its first acts was to rescind the armistice proclamation, ensuring that Hungary remained in the Axis camp until the last days of the war.

Left: Waffen-SS troops — probably 7th SS Gebirgs Division Prinz Eugen — in Split after retaking the town from partisans in 1943. Note the ancient Renault R35 tanks. The fighting in Yugoslavia against Tito's partisans was tough, uncompromising and studded with atrocities.

Below left: The Russian troop positions at the time of 'Panzerfaust', and (inset) Castle Hill in Budapest.

BUDAPEST 1944

The scene of one of Skorzeny's most brilliant triumphs, the effect of Operation 'Panzerfaust' was only to delay the inevitable. The Russians were on the doorstep, and Hungary would fall to them, no matter who was in power. The Soviet army completed the encirclement of the city on Christmas Eve 1944. Up till then the city had survived the war largely intact: during the 108-day siege, most of it would be destroyed. Pest, on one side of the Danube, was liberated by Soviet troops first, on 14 January 1945, while Buda held out for another month against the Soviet advance. The taking of the Royal Castle and the caves beneath it was a massacre. When it was over, the population of Budapest had fallen to 833,000 some 28% less than in 1941. Only a quarter of the buildings were intact.

Above: The *leichter Ladungsträger* SdKfz 302/303 Goliath. See pages 74–5 for technical details. *IWM B5115*

Below: A Goliath team prepares to set their vehicle on its way. First the two-wheel trailer is detached. *via Chris Ellis*

OPERATION '*GREIF*' — SKORZENY AND THE BULGE

Skorzeny's stock was riding high with Hitler after the swoop on Budapest and the Führer summoned him to an awards' ceremony at Rastenburg, his headquarters hidden deep in the forest of East Prussia, on 22 October. The commando leader was raised to the rank of SS-Obersturmbannführer (lieutenant-colonel) and was also briefed on his part in the forthcoming Operation '*Wacht am Rhein*' ('Watch on the Rhine'), better known as the Battle of the Bulge. Hitler was planning an all-out blow against the Allies marshalled along the west German border and the plan was to deploy the best of his remaining troops in the wooded Ardennes, from where the fall of France in 1940 had been engineered, and unleash them against the understrength, green and exhausted US troops holding a sector of the front stretching from Monschau in Belgium southward to Echternach in Luxembourg. After the initial breakthrough, which it was hoped would drive a wedge between the US forces and the British to the north, the German spearhead was to swing to the northwest and strike out for Antwerp, the most important forward supply port held by the Allies. Crucial to the plan was the need to seize bridges over the River Meuse (Maas) between Liege and Namur and roughly half way between the first point of attack and final objective. Speed was of the essence and Hitler had devised a plan to take the bridges by subterfuge, by deploying a special unit of men with US equipment and wearing GI clothing. Skorzeny was informed that he had to raise and lead this new force, which was designated the 150th Panzer Brigade, and that it would be deployed on the northern wing of '*Wacht am Rhein*' as part of Gen Sepp Dietrich's Sixth SS Panzer Army. Hitler also stressed that the target bridges had to be secured no more than 24 hours after the opening of the offensive, which was initially scheduled for early December but was later pushed back to the 16th.

According to Hitler's original timetable Skorzeny had little more than five weeks to find sufficiently competent English speakers and train them for their part in 'Wacht am Rhein', which was codenamed Operation 'Greif' (Griffon). Within a few days of the meeting, he sent Gen Alfred Jodl, chief of staff of the OKW, a list of his requirements, which included some 3,300 men to form the three battalions that would be the core of the 150th Panzer Brigade. OKW passed the request on to Oberkommando West (Ob West), the body responsible for the the conduct of the direct war in Western Europe, on 25 October and it in its turn sent the order down the chain of command to the various army groups in the theatre. In a worrying breach of security, the repeated requests sent to the army groups were intercepted by the Allies but it appears the information was not acted upon as their high command doubted that Germany was militarily capable of launching a major offensive on the Western Front.

Skorzeny soon became aware that little US equipment was finding its way to his new command and on 2 November he contacted Ob West's chief of staff, Lt-Gen Siegfried Westphal, to demand a greater effort. A week later Ob West sent out orders to the army groups under its command to provide the captured Allied uniforms, small arms, ammunition and heavier equipment that Skorzeny had requested, including 15 tanks, 20 self-propelled guns, 20 armoured cars, 120 trucks, 100 jeeps and 40 motorcycles. The operation to gather the war matériel was codenamed 'Rabenhügel' (Raven's Hill) and each army group was allotted a particular quota of tanks and jeeps. Army Group B had to provide five tanks and 30 jeeps, Army Group G eight tanks and 20 jeeps and Army Group H two tanks and 50 jeeps. The equipment was supposed to be delivered to the panzer brigade's training base at Grafenwöhr but it quickly became apparent to Skorzeny that his targets were not being met. He complained to Ob West on the 21st but matters did not improve to any extent and he had to improvise by hastily transforming German equipment. The silhouettes of Panther tanks were modified by the addition of steel turret plates cut to give them the profile of US M10 tank-destroyers (see colour section, pages 70–1) but most of the other German heavy equipment received nothing more than an overall coat of US olive drab camouflage paint and the Allied white star recognition symbol stencilled to their superstructures. A report sent to Ob West in late November revealed that the 150th Panzer Brigade roster of equipment totalled just 57 jeeps, 74 trucks and two armoured cars, a third of which were in poor condition and needed overhauling by the unit's mechanics. Two Shermans had turned up but both proved unserviceable and, most bizarrely, Skorzeny also received considerable quantities of former Polish or Russian equipment. US uniforms also proved a problem as the brigade was short of 1,500 steel helmets and many of the uniforms were summer rather than winter issue.

Skorzeny was also having problems finding suitably qualified men to take on the role of US troops. Language experts scoured the German armed forces for suitable candidates but after two weeks their efforts were less than impressive. Ten men, mostly sailors, were discovered who had a high proficiency in American English and a good command of slang; 30 to 40 more were found to speak convincingly but had little or no knowledge of slang; around 150 men spoke English to an adequate degree, and some 200 had studied English at school during their youth. Skorzeny was dubious as to their value and later remarked that, 'In practice it meant that we might as well just mingle with the fleeing Americans and pretend to be too flurried and overcome to speak.'

The difficulties of locating suitable men and equipment impacted on Skorzeny's original mission for the panzer brigade and he had to scale down his plans: rather than having three battalions he would have to make do with just two. Each was supposed to

THE IMPACT OF *EINHEIT STIELAU*

It is difficult to assess the military value of the English-speaking *Stielau* detachments during the Battle of the Bulge. It seems that the scale of their operations has been exaggerated, partly because of Skorzeny's own embellishment of the facts and partly because nervous US troops frequently reported incursions by German soldiers that were subsequently attributed to *Stielau* groups. Equally an enemy soldier wearing partial US clothing was a not uncommon sight in the winter of 1944–45 due to the increasingly wretched and poorly quality uniforms provided, if at all, by German manufacturers. Skorzeny provided some details of *Stielau* activities but many other details are based on personal recollections from US soldiers and local civilians. For example, one Belgian civilian reported overhearing a German-speaking US officer at Lingueville on 16 December; the following day US Sgt Edward Keoghan reported being stuck in a traffic jam outside Malmédy and a conversation with a MP who stated that the roads signs had been switched to send US troops in the wrong direction; and Sgt John Myers recorded a *Stielau* team being killed at Poteau on the 18th after betraying themselves through their ignorance of the subtleties of US Army unit designations. One of the *Stielau* men claimed they were from Company E of a cavalry unit when in fact cavalry units used the term troop. It is also a matter of official record that one three-man team was captured at Aywaille on the 17th after giving the wrong password. In his own writing Skorzeny states that the last *Stielau* team was sent through US lines on the 19th after which they reverted to wearing German uniforms as the element of surprise had been lost.

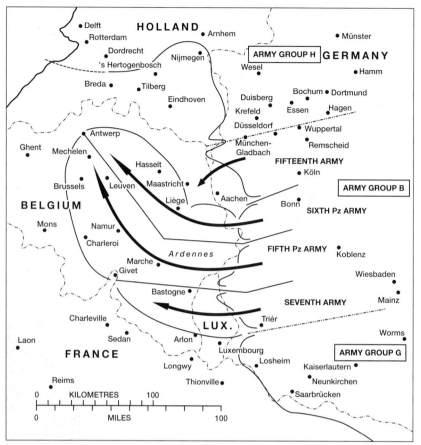

Above: Hitler's plan — push through the Ardennes to Brussels and Antwerp, split the Allied armies into two and finish them off individually.

Above right: Within a few hours of meeting Hitler on 22 October, Skorzeny sent Gen Alfred Jodl, chief of staff of the OKW, a list of his requirements. Jodl passed it down the chain of command on 25 October and did little to pursue the matter. The result was that Skorzeny had nowhere near sufficient men, vehicles or supplies to undertake his mission. *via George Forty*

Below right: On 2 November Skorzeny contacted Ob West's chief of staff, Lt-Gen Siegfried Westphal seen here in the Western desert, to demand a greater effort. It took a week before Ob West sent out orders that Skorzeny should be provided with the equipment he had requested. By this time there was absolutely no chance that he would be able to complete his mission. *via George Forty*

consist of four infantry companies, a company of armoured cars, a single AA platoon and a company of tanks. The 1st Battalion was allocated 22 PzKpfw V Panthers, and an additional company of Panzergrenadiers, while the 2nd Battalion was to be provided with 14 StuG IIIs. Additional units attached to the brigade also included a company of engineers, bridge-building detachments and a battery of self-propelled guns. However, It soon became apparent that even these plans were overly ambitious and at the last minute Skorzeny was again forced to reorganise the men and equipment he had available. Finally assembled at Grafenwöhr were 2,500 troops, some 1,200 from the army, 800 from Luftwaffe ground units and 500 from the Waffen-SS — a total of 800 men short of his original figure — and the organisation of the brigade was modified for the second time, resulting in three battle groups. SS Lt-Col Willi Hardieck took charge of Kampfgruppe X, Kampfgruppe Y was placed under Capt Scherff, and Kampfgruppe Z devolved to Lt-Col Wolf. In their final form each battle group comprised three infantry companies, two panzergrenadier platoons, two mortar platoons along with engineer, signals and mechanical detachments. Kampfgruppen X and Y also received additional armour in the shape of five Panthers modified to look like M10s and five StuG III assault guns respectively. Each battle group was assigned to one of the main assault divisions of Dietrich's Sixth SS Panzer Army.

The shortage of top-grade English speakers had also resulted in a rethink. The best were formed into a commando detachment known as *Einheit Stielau* (Unit Stielau), which would be the most 'American' of Skorzeny's forces, but as none of these recruits had any experience of such missions, all had to undergo a period of brief but intensive training in explosive and radio transmission as well as learning about US rank badges and drill. Some were sent to prisoner of war camps at Küstrin and Limburg to improve their English and get up to speed on US slang. *Einheit Stielau* was split into several small detachments each with a specific task. Some were formed into teams of five or six to carry out sabotage missions against ammunition depots, bridges and fuel dumps; others, usually three or four men in jeeps, were to head for the Meuse to reconnoitre the way forward and at the same time spread alarm and confusion among US units they met. Finally, detachments of three to four men were assigned individually to the divisions for which the panzer brigade was acting as a spearhead. Their chief role was to undermine the US command structure by destroying radio stations, issuing false orders and severing telephone wires.

As the date for Operation '*Wacht am Rhein*' approached, Skorzeny finally revealed the brigade's role to his three battle group commanders on 10 December. He stated that they had to take intact at least two of three bridges over the Meuse at Amay, Andenne and Huy. In the first hours of the attack they were to keep pace with but travel slightly behind the leading elements of the main assault divisions to preserve the special unit's anonymity until they had reached an area known as the Hohes Venn — a line running approximately southwest to northeast centred on the small town of Spa about 20 miles (32km) from their start point around Losheim and a similar distance from the Meuse to the northwest. Once the Hohes Venn had been reached the three groups were to strike out on their own along parallel routes and, travelling under cover of darkness, reach the bridges within six hours. Skorzeny stressed that to ensure the success of the operation Hohes Venn had to be reached on the first day of 'Wacht am Rhein' and the bridges secured early on the second.

Shortly after this briefing the brigade moved out of its camp at Grafenwöhr and, travelling only at night to avoid detection, arrived at Münstereifel on 14 December. Two days later the offensive opened at 0530 hours and the three Kampfgruppen advanced in conjunction with the lead elements of three divisions of Gen Hermann Priess's 1st SS Panzer Corps — Brig Wilhelm Mohnke's 1st SS Panzer Division Leibstandarte Adolf Hitler, the 12th SS Panzer Division Hitlerjugend and the 12th Volksgrenadier Division — to which they had been attached. Skorzeny accompanied his brigade's Kampfgruppe X, which was detailed to operate with a battle group under Lt-Col Jochen Peiper drawn from the Leibstandarte. The attack called for the utmost speed yet quickly became bogged down due to the appalling weather and the area's poor roads and weak bridges that could not cope with the mass of vehicles that the German were trying to pass down them. The greatest bottleneck was around the Losheim Gap, virtually on the offensive's startline, and it was here also that Kampfgruppe X suffered the loss of its commander, Hardieck, who fell victim to a mine. His replacement was

Above: A PzKpfw V Panther tank tries to get past a column of halftracks in the snowclad Ardennes, highlighting vividly the chaos resulting from traffic congestion. In the end a combination of lack of men and equipment, chronic traffic jams and bad weather meant that Panzer Brigade 150 was forced to fight in a conventional role. *RAC Tank Museum via George Forty*

Above right: The Brandenburgers' war in the west had started with the Meuse (Maas) bridges in 1940: the bridges were also the intended targets for Skorzeny's commandos during the Battle of the Bulge. This map, based on one produced by the air reconnaissance office, shows the information about the bridges known to the Germans on 12 December — the dates identify the most recent photos available. When Hitler briefed Skorzeny he emphasised the need to seize bridges between Liege and Namur.

a former Brandenburg officer and Knight's Cross holder, Baron Adrian von Foelkersam, now a captain in the Waffen-SS. Matters did not improve over the next few hours and it was rapidly becoming clear to Skorzeny that the collapse of the original timetable was critically undermining Operation 'Greif'. He might have had an even gloomier prognosis of the deteriorating situation if he had been aware that key documents relating to 'Greif' had been captured near Heckhuscheid by elements of the US 7th Armored Division.

Skorzeny acted to retrieve the situation during a night meeting on the 17th at the headquarters of the SS Sixth Panzer Army. He asked for, and was granted, permission to reform his three scattered battle groups as a single force and attach them to the 1st SS Panzer Division, which was currently headquartered at Ligneuville. The 150th Panzer Brigade was ordered to assemble there and participate in the division's general attack towards the still-distant Meuse. Its chief objective was to take Malmédy, a key position where two roads, one running north–south and the other east–west, met. Capture of the small town a few miles to the north of Ligneuville would threaten the western flank of the divisions of Maj-Gen Leonard Gerow's US V Corps holding the Elsenborn Ridge to the east that were blocking the advance of the Hitlerjugend and also aid Kampfgruppe Peiper, which was struggling to maintain the momentum on its assigned route of advance some way to the south of Malmédy. Skorzeny planned his assault on the basis that Malmédy was weakly held — one of his commando teams had briefly entered the village during the 17th to discover its defenders were just a few US engineers — but did not know that the position had later received reinforcements in the shape of the US 30th Infantry Division's 120th Infantry Regiment and the 99th Infantry Battalion. To Skorzeny's annoyance he had to draw up a plan of attack on 20 December on the basis that his Kampfgruppe Z would not reach the brigade's two other battle groups in time because of the clogged roads. Consequently only Kampfgruppe X, attacking from

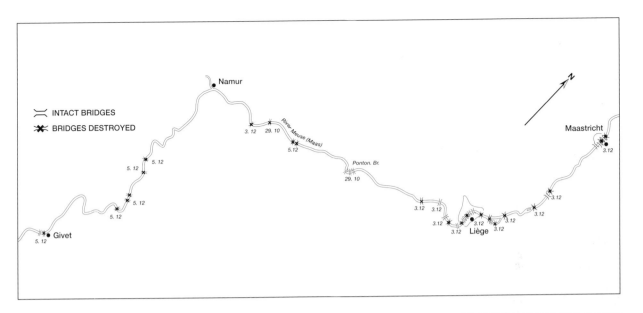

INTACT BRIDGES

BRIDGES DESTROYED

Namur

Maastricht
3.12

River Meuse (Maas)

3. 12   29. 10

5.12

5. 12

5. 12

Ponton. Br.
29. 10

5. 12

3.12   3.12

3.12

5. 12

3.12   3.12
3.12   Liège   3.12

Givet
5. 12

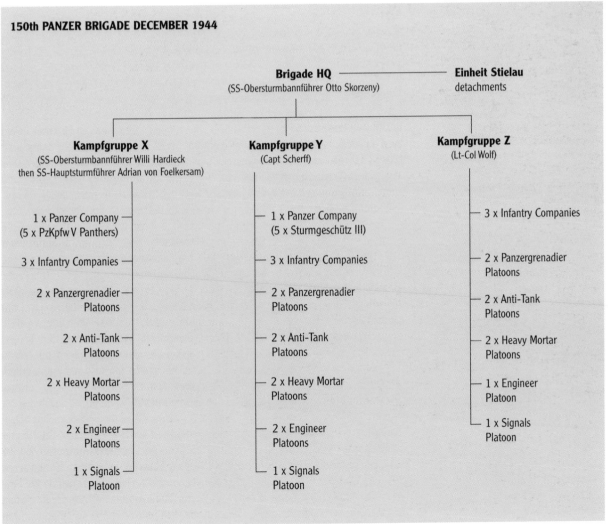

150th PANZER BRIGADE DECEMBER 1944

Brigade HQ —————— **Einheit Stielau**
(SS-Obersturmbannführer Otto Skorzeny)   detachments

Kampfgruppe X
(SS-Obersturmbannführer Willi Hardieck
then SS-Hauptsturmführer Adrian von Foelkersam)

Kampfgruppe Y
(Capt Scherff)

Kampfgruppe Z
(Lt-Col Wolf)

Kampfgruppe X	Kampfgruppe Y	Kampfgruppe Z
1 x Panzer Company (5 x PzKpfw V Panthers)	1 x Panzer Company (5 x Sturmgeschütz III)	3 x Infantry Companies
3 x Infantry Companies	3 x Infantry Companies	2 x Panzergrenadier Platoons
2 x Panzergrenadier Platoons	2 x Panzergrenadier Platoons	2 x Anti-Tank Platoons
2 x Anti-Tank Platoons	2 x Anti-Tank Platoons	2 x Heavy Mortar Platoons
2 x Heavy Mortar Platoons	2 x Heavy Mortar Platoons	1 x Engineer Platoon
2 x Engineer Platoons	2 x Engineer Platoons	1 x Signals Platoon
1 x Signals Platoon	1 x Signals Platoon	

Above: A Sturmgeschütz III of Kampfgruppe Y, abandoned beside the N32 at Géromont. Pictured on 15 January, while US troops remove a booby trap, note the Allied markings. *US Army*

Above right: GIs of 393rd Infantry Regiment, 99th Infantry Division, digging in on Elsenborn Ridge on 19 December – before the snows came – and came – and came! *US Army via George Forty*

Below right: Sturmgeschütz III — Kampfgruppe Y had five that went into action on the 21st, running into the 120th Infantry on the N32. *via George Forty*

Below: One of Kampfgruppe X's five disguised Panthers. *La Gleize Museum*

Ligneuville, and Kampfgruppe Y, pushing on Malmédy from Baugnez, were committed to the pincer attack. The third battle group would be held in reserve if it arrived in time. The advance was scheduled to begin early on the 21st and Skorzeny hoped that speed and surprise would make up for his unit's depleted strength and lack of heavy artillery. Once again, as at Heckhuscheid, his plans were compromised when one of his men was captured on the afternoon of the 20th and revealed that Malmédy was earmarked for attack the next day.

Kampfgruppe Y moved off from Baugnez under cover of night early on the 21st, advancing down one of the region's better roads, the N32, but soon ran into the alert outposts of the US 120th Infantry Regiment. Hit by tremendous artillery fire the group's attack stalled and it soon withdrew back to its start line. Kampfgruppe X, which was led by five disguised Panthers and two infantry companies, moved forward from Ligneuville along the Route de Falize and, after passing through Bellevaux, ran into positions held by the 120th's 3rd Battalion to the west of Malmédy at 0430 hours. The battle group now split in two. The greater part turned left and advanced down a small road that led to a bridge over the Warche River, while the smaller portion pushed directly on to Malmédy along the Route de Falize. The troops heading for the bridge set off US-laid trip wires that sent illuminating flares into the dark sky, revealing the silhouettes of the accompanying Panthers. The tanks immediately opened fire but US tank destroyers, firing from the cover of a house close to the bridge, checked the German armour. The accompanying panzergrenadiers made a rush for the house but the 30 men inside, members of the 291st Engineers and Company K, 120th Regiment, beat them off after a vicious close-quarters firefight. However, the attack on the house allowed the Panthers to resume their advance and one gained a position on the bridge where it was able to kill the crews of the US tank destroyers. As the battle around the Warche bridge developed, the other element of the battle group was facing an equally tough struggle. Led toward Malmédy by its own Panthers, the remainder of Kampfgruppe X was halted by a minefield sown at the foot of a railway embankment. One of the tanks soon brewed up and the accompanying panzergrenadiers launched several unsuccessful attacks to dislodge the defenders, Company B of the US 99th Infantry Battalion. The fight ebbed and flowed but the German troops were finally forced to retire under a heavy barrage from US artillery based on high ground to the north of the Werthe river. Using shells fitted with the newly developed proximity fuse set to airburst, they caused several casualties among the panzergrenadiers.

By around 1030 hours the early morning fog that had clouded the two battlefields around Malmédy cleared, allowing the US forces at the Warche bridge and on the railway embankment to see each other for the first time. Aided by the clearer weather the US artillery continued its deluge of shells, firing some 3,000 rounds by the time the action ebbed away over the next few hours. The Panther holding the bridge was destroyed and the others found it impossible to make any headway. Skorzeny, watching the deteriorating situation from high ground on the Route de Falize, saw that the game

Right: It is easy with hindsight to write off the Ardennes offensive as the squandering of German reserves that would have been better spent in defence of the Reich. Indeed, the Battle of the Bulge took the eyes away from the vicious battles going on in the Hürtgen Forest — attritional warfare that favoured the defenders. Nevertheless, counterattack was part of German military doctrine, and there was no doubting the quality of their troops nor their commitment to the cause — as evinced by this group. It is a well-known, probably posed, photograph from a sequence showing troops from the 2nd Company, SS-Panzergrenadier Regiment 1. *US Army*

Opposite, Above: The confusion created by the 'Greif' teams was widespread and far reaching: everyone took much more care to identify units and individuals when they could. Here US 84th Infantry Division MPs check vehicles at the Baillonville crossroads in Marche, Belgium. *US Army via TRH Pictures*

Opposite, Below: In the end the offensive simply dissipated Germany's meagre resources and hastened the end of the war. *US Army*

Below: This photograph shows two German soldiers looting dead US troops (note the lack of boots on corpse at left). *US Army*

was up and the surviving Panthers were ordered to cover the withdrawal of the panzergrenadiers. By mid-afternoon Kampfgruppe X was back at the start point on the high ground south of the Werthe with its commander, Foelkersam, nursing a painful wound in his posterior. Skorzeny had also been wounded by a shell splinter that caught him in the face as he returned to the Leibstandarte's headquarters at Ligneuville to discuss the deteriorating situation at Malmédy. The wounds inflicted on Skorzeny and Foelkersam did not prevent one final push on Malmédy by Kampfgruppe Y in the early hours of the 22nd but the advance soon bogged down in the face of resistance from the 120th Regiment. Members of the 291st Engineers also added to the difficulties facing the attackers by blowing the Warche bridge as well as a rail bridge over the N32, which severed the main road east of Malmédy, and a second railway bridge that crossed the Route de Falize. Skorzeny returned to the battlefront on the 23rd after having had his wound dressed but quickly recognised that the Meuse bridges were permanently beyond the reach of his battered command, particularly as Allied reinforcements were being rushed to the area.

The panzer brigade's involvement in 'Wacht am Rhein' ended when it was relieved by the 18th Volksgrenadier Division

Key players in the Ardennes in 1944:

Opposite, Above right: SS-Gruppenführer Hermann Priess commanded Ist SS Panzer Corps, to which Skorzeny's *Kampfgruppen* were attached.

Left and Below: Two photographs of Joachim 'Jochen' Peiper. The first (**Left**) shows him as an SS-Sturmbannführer at Kursk in 1943 while commanding the IIIrd Battalion of Leibstandarte's 2nd SS Panzergrenadier Regiment in one of the crucial Eastern Front battles. In the other, autumn 1944, photograph (**Below**) he has been promoted to SS-Obersturmbannführer. He wears a black SS Panzer uniform and a Knight's Cross with Oakleaves. Note the 'Leibstandarte' cuff title. Kampfgruppe X was detailed to operate with a Leibstandarte battle group under Peiper. *TRH Pictures*

Opposite, above left and Below left: SS-Obergruppenführer und Gen der Waffen-SS 'Sepp' Dietrich, commander of Sixth SS Panzer Army. He is seen here wearing the Waffen-SS winter dress and his Knight's Cross with Oakleaves. He would go on to become one of only two members of the Waffen-SS to be awarded the Diamonds to add to the Oakleaves and Swords. A rough, tough 'bully boy', who lacked military knowledge, he was nevertheless a brave and fearless individual, much respected by his troops. *RAC Tank Museum via George Forty*

on the 28th and pulled back to Schlierback to the east of St Vith. It then moved by train to Grafenwöhr and was disbanded with the troops being returned to their original units by 23 January 1945. Skorzeny's force had had a brief existence, little more than three months, and had been in action for just under two weeks. It had a casualty rate of around 15 percent, mostly victims of Allied artillery strikes or the air attacks that intensified once the low cloud over the battle area began dispersing on the 23rd. The deception plan had involved several groups of men dressed in US uniforms and the last of these penetrated behind Allied lines on 19 December after which the element of surprise had been lost, the opposing US units alerted and the remainder reverted to wearing German uniforms. It is difficult to quantify the impact of '*Greif*' as much of the evidence is anecdotal. The teams undoubtedly added to the panic and uncertainty that gripped some US forces in the first days of the offensive and the rumour that their actual target was Eisenhower did restrict the Allied supreme commander's freedom of action as security was built up around him. The man who had started this rumour, L/Cpl Wilhelm Schmidt, was captured at Aywaille on 17 December with the two other members of a *Einheit Stielau* commando group, Oberfähnrich Günther Billing and Cpl Manfred Pernass, after failing to provide the right password. After a military trial, the three men were shot by

Above: The end of the 'Bulge'. A column of German prisoners passing a US Third Army tank. *US Army via George Forty*

Above left: A Tiger II passes a long line of Americans taken prisoner at the start of the offensive. *US Army via George Forty*

Left: American generals gather at 12th Army Group headquarters, Bad Wildungan, Germany, 12 May 1945. Gen Dwight D. Eisenhower, with some of his most senior American generals including, front row left to right, William H. Simpson (CG US Ninth Army), George S. Patton, Jr (CG US Third Army), Carl A. Spaatz (CG USATAF), Eisenhower (Supreme Commander), Omar N. Bradley (CG 12th Army Group), Courtney M. Hodges (CG US First Army), Leonard T. Gerow (CG US Fifteenth Army). It was Gerow's V Corps that held the Elsenborn Ridge and bore the brunt of the attack by Kampfgruppe Peiper and the Hitlerjugend Division. *US Army via George Forty*

Right: The massacre of Malmédy is revealed. The events of 17 December 1944 would lead to a war crimes trial in which Skorzeny and his men were convicted but later acquitted. While there were undoubtedly premeditated atrocities during the Battle of the Bulge, it is difficult to say what triggered the events at Malmédy. *US Army via TRH Pictures*

firing squad on the 23rd at Henri-Chapelle (see photo on page 68) and their fate was shared by 15 other men of the *Stielau* teams, who were executed at either Henri-Chapelle or Huy.

SKORZENY'S LAST BATTLES

Germany's military situation deteriorated rapidly after the collapse of '*Wacht am Rhein*' but Skorzeny was still called on for special missions, although many of his forces were committed to conventional ground operations and would be bled white by the time of Germany's surrender. In January 1945 he sent several groups of Russian-speaking Germans and Russian turncoats deep behind the advancing Red Army to aid trapped German units attempting to reach friendly territory. Several teams were flown deep behind the Soviet lines into the western Soviet union in aircraft operated by KG 200, but most disappeared without trace and only one eventually linked up with a 2,000-strong group of troops from several units under the command of Lt-Col Scherhorn.

Skorzeny requested that Scherhorn make his way to some frozen lakes some 200 miles (320km) from Minsk, from where the trapped men could be airlifted to safety. It took Scherhorn several weeks to reach the lakes but there was no rescue as Germany lacked the aircraft and fuel to undertake such a long-range mission on the scale required.

At the end of January Skorzeny was ordered to assemble his forces around Schwedt on the Oder River to block the massive Soviet offensive toward Berlin. The fighting was vicious and consumed the greater part of his command by the end of February. As the Third Reich crumbled further in the final spring of the war Skorzeny returned to Berlin on 8 March and was ordered to destroy the Remagen bridge over the Rhine that had been captured by US troops the previous day. He immediately returned to Friedenthal and asked for volunteers from among the ranks of his Danube Frogman Group to destroy the bridge with explosive charges. They tried but failed with many dying from wounds or drowning after contracting frostbite in the bitterly cold waters of the Rhine.

Skorzeny was awarded the Knight's Cross with Oak Leaves in late March, when he spoke briefly to Hitler for the last time, and was then ordered to travel to Vienna to oversee the creation of the so-called Alpine Redoubt. The half-hearted scheme to establish this final centre of resistance was overtaken by Hitler's death and Germany's surrender, events that marked the end of the career of the 'most dangerous man in Europe' and Germany's special forces in World War II.

Right: US troops flood over the bridge at Remagen. Skorzeny's Danube Frogman Group tried unsuccessfully to blow the bridge in the last spring of the war. *US Army via George Forty*

Below: The 'Greif' commandos managed to create a good deal confusion and panic – but any Germans found driving jeeps could expect trouble. *US Signal Corps*

INSIGNIA, CLOTHING & EQUIPMENT

Neither the Brandenburgers nor Skorzeny's various commands were notably different from other German units in terms of the uniforms worn or the equipment carried as standard. Most photographs of the Brandenburgers show them wearing standard army clothing and insignia. However, due to the nature of their more clandestine operations they did make use of unusual German equipment and clothing that was far from standard issue among the Wehrmacht.

BADGES AND INSIGNIA

The Brandenburgers and Skorzeny's units wore standard issue clothing and insignia, as would be found among regular army or Waffen-SS forces. When not wearing foreign military dress or civilian clothing, the Brandenburgers were remarkably similar to any other German soldier with the exception of a cuff title. This was worn on on the lower left sleeve of the tunic and consisted of a band of dark green cloth with silver-grey thread, which was used for piping above and below the title *Brandenburg* rendered in gothic script. The title was worn throughout the war and Brandenburgers were still identifiable as such even when incorporated into the Grossdeutschland Panzer Corps in the final part of the war. The Panzergrenadier Division Brandenburg also had a distinctive field sign That was painted on to vehicles. This comprised a stylised eagle, the emblem of Brandenburg, superimposed on a white M1943 helmet shown in profile — the field sign of the Grossdeutschland Division. By linking the two insignia it indicated that the Panzergrenadier Division Brandenburg was part of the Grossdeutschland Panzer Corps.

Right: Tactical signs associated with the Brandenburgers: 1 Divisional Signals Battalion. 2 The sign of the Koenen Tropical Company. 3 Divisional vehicle marking combining Brandenburg eagle with Grossdeutschland Panzer Corps helmet. 4 Parachute Battalion.

Below right: The Brandenburgers and Skorzeny's SS commandos wore standard uniforms most of the time. Here Skorzeny sports the collar patches of an SS-Sturmbannführer; note the Nazi eagle and swastika badge worn by the SS on left upper arm; other uniformed bodies wore it on the left breast. *Bundesarchiv*

Below: Brandenburg Division cuff title.

Brandenburg

1

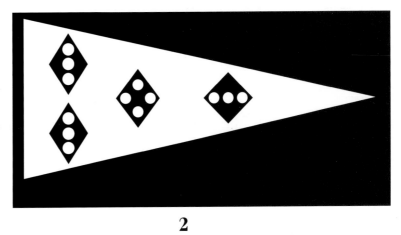

2

3

4

Right: Captured Germans (in this case probably *Greif* commandos) in Allied uniforms could well be shot as spies. *IWM PL 68548*

Below: American MPs tie Unteroffizier Manfred Pernass to the execution stake at Henri-Chapelle at dawn on 23 December 1944. Pernass and two other members of Skorzeny's *Einheit Stielau* – Oberfähnrich Günther Billing and Corporal Wilhelm Schmidt – were captured together wearing US Army uniforms and were subsequently executed together.
US Army via TRH Pictures

CLOTHING

There was nothing especially unique or unusual about the uniforms wore by either the Brandenburgers or Skorzeny's special forces. As is often the case, there was probably some relaxing of the strict dress regulations that were adhered to in more conventional units. There was undoubtedly greater variety in the case of the various Brandenburger detachments, some of which wore German paratrooper kit, tropical issue uniforms and clothing associated with mountain units. In general a detachment's specialisation, mission or area of operation would determine what clothing was appropriate. On Leros in late 1943 the Brandenburger paratroopers wore Luftwaffe tropical kit, while anti-partisan groups in the Balkans were seen in the cold-weather uniforms normally associated with mountain and Jäger units.

One area in which both the Brandenburgers and Skorzeny's forces were virtually unique during World War II was in the wearing of enemy uniforms, particularly in the case of the former, when conducting combat missions. Between 1939 and 1942 the Brandenburgers certainly wore them in Poland, Denmark, the Low Countries, North Africa and the Soviet Union and may have done so in the Balkans, but thereafter this ruse appears to have been little used by them. Skorzeny's men mostly famously wore foreign uniforms in one operation, that of the 150th Panzer Brigade and the *Stielau* detachment during Operation '*Wacht am Rhein*' in late 1944, but undoubtedly wore the military uniforms of other states as well as civilian clothes. Skorzeny himself went undercover during Operation '*Panzerfaust*' in 1944 and in his memoirs he records his troops wearing both Hungarian and civilian dress in the final weeks of the war.

Uniforms were sourced in several ways. The Brandenburgers bought Dutch uniforms in second-hand shops or made use of supplies captured by the Finns from the Red Army during the Winter War of 1939–40, while Skorzeny's forces in the Ardennes simply wore uniforms found in captured US supply dumps by other German troops. In the Brandenburgers' case the deceptions were mostly successful and for Skorzeny's men rather less so. It is wrong to believe that wearing the enemy's uniform effectively makes the wearer liable to summary execution. This is not the case in military law as a soldier may wear a captured uniform but only becomes liable to summary justice if he fights in it. Evidence indicates that at least on some occasions, Brandenburgers took off enemy greatcoats and headgear before going into action in the German uniforms worn beneath, but it seems equally likely that they also fought in partial or total enemy kit. We also know that Skorzeny's men in the Ardennes wore partial or complete US uniforms. The subtlties of this fine distinction in international military law were often lost in the heat of battle or simply unknown to ordinary front-line soldiers. It is well documented that 18 of the *Stielau* detachment were captured, tried and executed by firing squad for wearing US uniforms, although doubts have been cast over the legitimacy of the court's decision as it seems that in certain cases the men had not used their weapons. Nevertheless, German special forces captured in complete enemy uniforms were treated as spies and therefore liable for the death penalty.

The Brandenburgers and Skorzeny's commandos had very little specialised equipment. However, in the Ardennes in December 1944 Panzer Brigade 150 was intended to be equipped with Allied vehicles. In the event these proved difficult to get hold of; indeed, Skorzeny's intended allocation of 15 tanks, 20 SP guns and 20 armoured cars ended up being five Sturmgeschütz IIIs with Allied markings and five PzKpfw V Panthers made to look like Allied M10 tank destroyers by the addition of sheets of armour plate — as illustrated in this artwork which has been given US 10th Tank Battalion, 5th Armored Division markings.

Above: This Panther/M10 – coded 'B10' – shows how well disguised they were by use of appliqué plates, track links and Allied markings. *La Gleize Museum*

Below: 'B5' with 10th Tank Battalion, 5th Armored Division markings was knocked out by Sergeant Francis Currey who was awarded the Medal of Honor for his bravery on 21 December. *La Gleize Museum*

WEAPONS AND EQUIPMENT

Both Skorzeny's men and the Brandenburgers were generally lightly equipped for their operations and the small arms and few heavier support weapons they used on the majority of their missions were little different from the standard issue found in more conventional units. During their early spearhead missions between 1939 and 1942 the Brandenburgers went into action with nothing more than small arms and grenades, while Skorzeny's men appear to have been increasingly equipped with heavier machine

guns and mortars, as was the case with the 500th SS Parachute Battalion during its raid on Tito's headquarters during 1944. As the Brandenburgers expanded, they, too, received heavier equipment. In 1944, for example, the 3rd Battalion of the division's 2nd Regiment formed a light gun company. The Panzergrenadier Division *Brandenburg* was, of course, much more heavily equipped, including tanks and self-propelled guns, although it is doubtful that it ever fought at full strength given the parlous nature of Germany's armed forces in the final stages of the war.

Both the Brandenburgers and Skorzeny received items of foreign equipment. There is little firm evidence, but its seems like that they on occasion fought with the enemy's small arms. This was undoubtedly the case with Skorzeny's *Stielau* detachments during the Battle of the Bulge as these English-speaking units needed enemy small arms to complete their disguise as US troops. It is much more certain that they both regularly used foreign transport as seen by the Brandenburgers' use of Red Army trucks on the Eastern Front during 1941 and 1942 and Skorzeny's deployment of dozens of US jeeps during Operation '*Wacht am Rhein*'. The use of heavier vehicles, tanks and the like, is more debatable. All that can be said for sure is that Skorzeny tried to get US armour for Operation '*Greif*' but little was provided — just two unreliable Shermans that were not taken into action. If Skorzeny required heavier equipment for a mission it was usually provided by other units in his area of operations as was the case with the handful of Panther tanks that served under him during the coup in Budapest.

Occasionally the German special forces did receive items of equipment that were at the cutting edge of World War II technology. One of the best examples was the deployment of the Goliath during Operation '*Panzerfaust*'. This was a small tracked explosive device with the rhomboid profile of a World War I British tank (see pages 74–5). The device was powered by a petrol or electric engine and steered to its target by a trailing wire. Once the objective had been reached, the Goliath's 200lb (90kg) explosive charge could be detonated by remote control. It had a range of approximately 700 yards (640m) and a top speed under ideal conditions of around 10mph (16kph). The Goliath was not a great success. Its lack of range, slow speed and high profile meant that many were knocked out before reaching their intended target. During '*Panzerfaust*' Skorzeny intended to use the Goliath company attached to his command to destroy barricades but it seems they were not need as the faster-moving tanks could destroy or crush the obstacles more quickly.

Both the Brandenburgers and Skorzeny's men did make considerably more use of aircraft in their operations than conventional units. Among the types used were the Fieseler Fi156 *Storch* (Stork), a small short take-off and landing aircraft normally used for reconnaissance work and the transport of generals on the battlefield, but also deployed by Skorzeny to whisk Mussolini away from Gran Sasso in 1943. Normally carrying a pilot and passenger, the Stork entered service in 1937 and some 2,550 were produced. It had a top speed of around 110mph (176kph) and a range of 230 miles (368km).

Gliders were also deployed by the special forces, most commonly the DFS 230. Produced by the German Research Institute for Gliding, this was a fabric-covered machine with a tubular fuselage. It carried a pilot, co-pilot and 10 troops or one ton of equipment. The troops sat astride a wooden bench down the centre of the fuselage when in flight and deployed through two doors, one port and one starboard, on landing. The pilot and co-pilot exited through the removable forward perspex windscreen. The DFS 230 could be towed at a maximum speed of 100mph (160kph), usually by Junkers Ju52 transports, and once released descended at a rate of around 240ft (75m) per minute, although the special forces often approached the landing zone at a much steeper angle for a shorter landing, as Skorzeny did during the Mussolini rescue mission. The

PREVENTING FRIENDLY FIRE DURING 'WACHT AM RHEIN'

As both the men and equipment of the 150th Panzer Brigade and the *Einheit Stielau* were disguised entirely — or at least in part — to represent the US Army, Skorzeny recognised that there was a real danger of his units being fired on by their own side as their missions placed them at the leading edge of the attack and even behind the front line. He attempted to minimise this risk in a number of ways. First, Skorzeny's men were ordered to paint white dots on objects such as houses and trees to mark their route so that follow-on forces would know that somewhere in front of them were units belong to Skorzeny's command. Second, the vehicles used in Operation '*Greif*' were marked by a small yellow triangle at the rear as a field recognition signal. Third, while on the move and not in action his armoured vehicles, tanks and the like, were to keep their guns pointing in a particular direction. Fourth, the men were to wear pink-red or blue scarves and quickly remove their steel helmets if they made contact with German forces. Finally, torches fitted with red or blue filters were to be flashed as a means of identification at night.

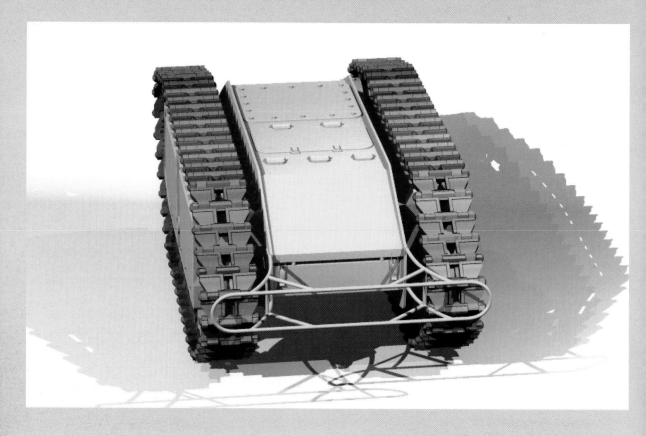

GOLIATH

The *leichter Ladungsträger* SdKfz 302/303 Goliath was an expendable remote-controlled tracked demolition charge was produced from 1942 to supersede the earlier *Minenräumwagen* (mine-clearance vehicle).

The Goliath was transported to the scene of action by a purpose-built two-wheeled trailer that could be pulled by two men or towed behind a vehicle. The attachment points are the holes in the centre of each side sponson and the bracket on the centreline of the hull front. The vehicle was remotely controlled via a three-strand cable that unwound from a drum in the rear compartment of the hull. (Two strands for guidance; one for detonation.) This led out via a slit opening through a guide cage that prevented the cable snagging on the tracks during tight turns. The compartment forward of this contained the electrical equipment for control and detonation, whilst at the front of the vehicle was the explosive charge — 60kg (132lb) — covered with a belt-down hatch. The side sponsons contained the batteries and two Bosch 2.5kW electric motors each connected via a short drive shaft to the transmission unit behind each sprocket.

There were three versions of the Goliath. Borgward and Zündapp produced 2,560 *E-motor* (electric-motor) SdKfz 302s between April 1942 and January 1944. It was succeeded by the V-motor (petrol-engined) SdKfz 303A. This was cheaper to produce and the more efficient petrol engine increased speed and range with a heavier payload of 75kg (165lb). This was the main production version and Zündapp and Zachertz produced 4,602 units between April 1943 and September 1944. This was in turn replaced in production by the SdKfz 303B in November 1944. Also petrol-engined, it was slightly larger than the 303A and could carry a charge of 100kg (220lb). By the end of the war 325 of this version had been built making a grand total of 7,487 of all types.

The main distinguishing feature between the electric and petrol-engined versions are:

a) top plate flat on 302; raised air intake on 303
b) three return rollers on 302; only two on 303
c) disc idler on 302; spoked idler on 303

	SdKfz 302	SdKfz 303A	SdKfz 303B
Weight (kg)	0.37	0.37	0.43
Length (m)	1.5	1.62	1.63
Width (m)	0.85	0.84	0.91
Height (m)	0.56	0.60	0.62
Speed (km/hr)	10	12	12
Range	650m of wire usually carried on drum		

Brandenburgers flew to some targets in the DFS 230 during the Tunisian campaign in 1943 and also apparently used the 24-ton Messerschmitt Me323 *Gigant* (Giant) glider on one occasion — the unsuccessful raid into Bucharest in 1944. Capable of carrying up to 120 troops, a tanks or 20 tons of supplies, this monster had to be towed by three tugs but the arrangement proved unsatisfactory. Consequently, rockets were fitted to aid the tugs during take off but these made little difference to the instability of the combination and later versions of the Gigant were converted to powered aircraft by the fitting of six engines. Some 200 Gigants were built but the design, the largest glider aircraft of the conflict, was generally unsatisfactory.

Although Skorzeny did have some involvement in naval special forces, his units mostly avoided amphibious warfare. This was not the case with the Brandenburgers, who established their own coastal raider battalion. Evidence is scarce but this battalion, which mostly served in the Adriatic and Aegean, was equipped with various sizes of powerful assault craft for carrying troops into action. At a lower level, it is known that the detachment that destroyed rail bridges on the Murmansk-Leningrad line in August 1942 made use of kayaks commandeered from pleasure boat businesses on Berlin's Wannsee that were fitted with small outboard motors for the raid. Some Brandenburgers were alarmed that they came in a range of rather bright colours — red, blue and orange — but they were used in the attack.

Above: Fieseler Storch liaison and observation aircraft as used on the Mussolini mission — although rather too small for the final number of passengers. *via George Forty*

Above left: Brandenburgers training for Operation 'Sealion' at Büsum in August 1940. Note the inflatable life jackets but otherwise standard equipment. *Bundesarchiv*

Left: The Germans used the DFS 230 assault glider from the start of the campaign in the west. The most famous escapade using DFS 230s was the capture of Fort Eban Emael on 10 May 1940. Its last significant use was delivering Otto Skorzeny's force for the rescue of Mussolini. *Bundesarchiv*

Centre left: Practice makes perfect — the Brandenburgers spent a great deal of time honing their skills ensuring that everyone knew what to do and when to do it.

Far left: The attack on Norway was spearheaded by lightly equipped Brandenburg and other special units. Note the number of hand grenades carried by these Marines. *Photo from* Signal *magazine.*

CABLE CAR TO VALLEY

HOTEL ALBERGO-RIFUGIO

STORCH TAKE-OFF RUN

CAMPO IMPERATORE VALLEY

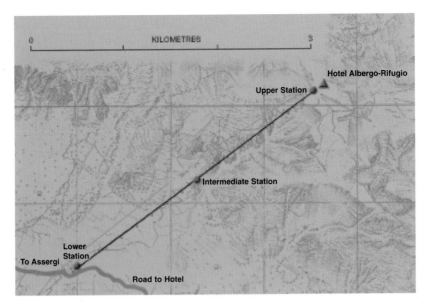

The freeing of Mussolini

This artwork shows (**left**) the mountain-top location of the hotel in which Mussolini was held and the take-off run of the Storch with (**above**) details of the funicular railway that ran up the Gran Sasso and (**below**) the location of the hotel in relation to Rome and central Italy.

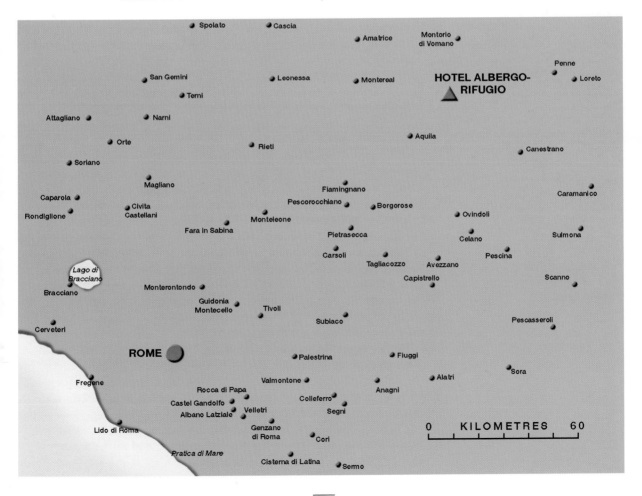

PEOPLE

WILHELM CANARIS (1887–1945)

Above: Admiral Canaris, who was head of the Abwehr from 1935. He did not devise the idea for the Brandenburg type of armed units and he was not entirely convinced of their usefulness, but nevertheless he accepted the idea. *Bundesarchiv*

Born into the family of a wealthy industrialist, Canaris joined the Imperial German Navy as a cadet in 1905 and during World War I served on board the *Dresden,* which fought in the battles of Coronel and the Falklands in November and December 1914. The cruiser escaped destruction but was eventually scuttled off Juan Fernandez on 14 March 1915, and Canaris made a daring escape back to Germany, avoiding internment and British agents on his trail. Canaris subsequently gained a reputation as an excellent intelligence officer during missions for the navy in Spain during 1915 and 1916, and in the final two years of the war he was a U-boat captain. In the interwar period he was a member of the military tribunal that tried the murderers of left-wing revolutionaries Karl Liebknecht and Rosa Luxembourg, who were killed during an attempted revolution in Berlin during January 1919. Over the following years he held several positions including that of captain of the predreadnought battleship *Schlesien* and was appointed head of the *Abwehr* in January 1935. He was responsible for organising military support for Francisco Franco during the Spanish Civil War. Between 1938 and 1940 Canaris was promoted vice-admiral and then admiral and made head of both the *Abwehr* and *Amt Ausland*. During this period the Brandenburgers were raised with his agreement

The admiral grew increasingly disillusioned with Hitler and from around 1938 became linked to various anti-Nazi resistance movements. The extent of his involvement is unclear but it seems he himself was opposed to any plans to kill Hitler and focused his efforts on protecting those around him who were more actively involved in anti-Nazi plots. Nevertheless Canaris was temporarily suspended from duty in February 1942 for aiding Jews to escape death in Germany by smuggling them to Switzerland. In March 1942 the *Abwehr* suffered two further blows: one of its officers, Paul Thümmel, was arrested and murdered by the Gestapo for supplying top secret information to Britain and the Soviet Union, and a British raid that successfully captured key parts of a German radar system at Bruneval on the north coast of France so enraged Hitler that he turned on the admiral and demanded to know why the *Abwehr* had singularly failed to uncover Britain's radar secrets. Henceforth the SS's intelligence and counter-espionage department took over much of the *Abwehr*'s work and Canaris appears to have sunk into apathy and despair.

Although the Gestapo suspected that he was negotiating with the Allies through neutral countries, the final blow came with the defection of an *Abwehr* officer in Istanbul, Erich Vermehren, to the British in early 1944. On 18 February, Hitler ordered the *Abwehr* dissolved, but Canaris was not arrested or imprisoned, merely temporarily suspended from duty until June when he was made chief of the department for economic warfare. The admiral was not directly involved in the July bomb plot to assassinate Hitler but one of those who was made mention of Canaris's name while being interrogated. Subsequent investigations discovered his personal diaries, which expressed strong anti-Nazi sympathies, and further details of his involvement in previous plots. Arrested, tried and convicted, he was taken to Flossenbürg concentration camp in Bavaria and executed on 9 April 1945.

HANS OSTER (1888–1945)

Oster was dismissed from the army because of an unacceptable love affair, but his fortunes improved when he joined the *Abwehr* in May 1933 and gained the confidence of its chief, Admiral Wilhelm Canaris. Canaris was able to engineer Oster's readmittance to the officer corps and made him his deputy in 1938. Oster was utterly opposed to Hitler and the Nazis and became involved in several conspiracies to remove him from power. In 1938 he joined an unsuccessful attempt to remove Hitler, and while some of the conspirators advocated that Hitler be simply deposed, Oster believed passionately that he had to be assassinated to break his grip over the will of the German people. Oster's position became less secure as the *Abwehr*'s fortunes declined and those of the SS rose but he continued to plot Hitler's downfall. In February 1943 he provided explosives for Col Henning von Tresckow, who with fellow officers planned but failed to

Above: Hans Oster.

kill Hitler when he visited Army Group Centre's headquarters at Smolensk. Oster was sacked a few weeks later after the Gestapo had found definitive evidence of his involvement in 'U-7' — an *Abwehr*-run operation that between late September and early December 1942 spirited away Jewish refugees from certain death in Germany to neutral Switzerland. His fate was sealed when he became implicated in the July 1944 bomb plot against Hitler. Arrested on 21 July, he was tried and conviction of treason and finally executed at Flossenbürg concentration camp on 9 April 1945.

ADRIAN VON FOELKERSAM (1914–45)

Born on 20 December 1914 in St Petersburg, Russia, the son of a Baltic German admiral who had served in the Russian Tsarist Navy and fought against the Japanese in the Russo-Japanese war of 1904–5, Adrian Baron von Foelkersam could speak fluent Russian, English and German and studied economics at universities in Berlin and Vienna. He joined the Brandenburgers in 1939 and took part in many operations. His greatest achievement — and the one for which he was awarded the Knight's Cross (on 14 September 1942) — was during the capture of the Maikop oilfields in the Caucasus when he was a lieutenant with the Ist Battalion of the Brandenburg Regiment. He and his men — 62 Baltic and Sudeten Germans, nicknamed the 'wild bunch' — disguised as Soviet troops, prevented the destruction of the oilfields by retreating Soviet forces. Using Red Army trucks and NKVD (Russian secret police) uniforms they infiltrated the Soviet lines and ran into a large group of Red Army deserters. Foelkersam persuaded them to return to the Soviet cause and this gave him the credentials he needed when he reached Maikop.

Below: Lt Adrian Baron von Foelkersam, seen wearing his newly awarded Knight's Cross. *Bundesarchiv*

Pretending to be a Major Truchin from Stalingrad, Foelkersam convinced the Russian general commanding the area that he was who he said he was; the general even gave him a personal tour of the city's defences. On 8 August, with the German army near, the Brandenburgers used grenades to simulate an artillery attack and knocked out the communications centre. Foelkersam then convinced the Russian defenders to withdraw and the German army was able to enter the city without a fight the next day.

When the Brandenburgers were formed into the Brandenburg Division and made part of the Grossdeutschland Panzer Corps, von Foelkersam — along with many other Brandenburgers — joined Skorzeny's new SS commando unit. Skorzeny accepted him with alacrity and he was promoted Oberleutnant, based at the unit's Friedenthal training ground where Skorzeny had set up his HQ.

Skorzeny's first mission — an attempt to kidnap Marshal Pétain — was cancelled; the second was the precursor to Operation '*Rösselsprung*' — the attack on Tito's headquarters (see pages 42–5) to kill or capture the Yugoslav partisan leader. Initially planned to involve only a small squad of men dressed as partisans, the plan escalated into a major operation, which involved the Waffen-SS 500th Parachute Battalion and other Army and Waffen-SS units. With little security, the partisans soon got wind of the operation and in the end Skorzeny and Foelkersam were lucky to escape with their lives.

Shortly afterwards Foelkersam was involved in the reaction to the 20 July Bomb Plot. During the confusion of the first few hours after the attempt on Hitler's life, Skorzeny and his men were among the many who stood firmly against the conspirators. Foelkersam was assigned to guard the SS intelligence building.

He took part in Skorzeny's brilliant Operation '*Panzerfaust*' (see pages 45–9) at the forefront of the action and his relationship with Skorzeny was further strengthened when Foelkersam became his adjutant.

During the Ardennes offensive Skorzeny's Panzer Brigade 150 was split into three Kampfgruppen — X, Y and Z (see pages 50–64) — and after the death of Kampfgruppe X commander SS-Obersturmbannführer Willi Hardieck, whose vehicle struck a land mine, Foelkersam took over the command. Kampfgruppe X took part in the actions around Malmédy, Ligneuville and Belleveux and engaged the US 3rd Battalion, 120th Regiment west of Malmédy.

With the failure of the Ardennes offensive Foelkersam went east again with SS-Jagdverband Ost, which was briefly under Skorzeny's command. As SS-Hauptsturmführer and Chief of Staff, Foelkersam asked for and was given the command of the unit. He had personal reasons for fighting the Russians — his brother had been captured by the Red Army and his wife and young daughter were living in the east near Posen. However, he did last long in his new command: he was killed by a head wound on 21 January 1945 near Hohensalza.

He was promoted posthumously to the rank of SS-Sturmbannführer and on 5 February received the *Ehrenblattspange des Heeres* (Roll of Honour clasp of the German Army).

Below: The Roll of Honour clasp of the German Army was instituted by Adolf Hitler on 30 January 1944 for exceptional bravery, that didn't quite reach the level required for the Knight's Cross. Over 4,500 had been awarded by war's end. Adrian Baron Foelkersam was awarded his pothumously.

THEODORE-GOTTLIEB VON HIPPEL

As has already been discussed in Origins and History (pages 9–10), the legacy of German Gen Paul von Lettow-Vorbeck's superb guerrilla war in East Africa made a profound mark upon one of his junior officers, a young captain named Theodore von Hippel. Finding a place in the German intelligence community after the war, Hippel proposed utilizing small, elite units to penetrate enemy defences before hostilities or offensive actions had begun. However, the idea ran afoul of the stiff-necked Prussian sense of honor. Hippel persevered, however, and when he became an officer in the war ministry's intelligence agency, the Abwehr, his ideas finally found a home.

Under Admiral Wilhelm Canaris, the German high command allowed Hippel to do what he had proposed — and thus the Brandenburgers were formed. Hippel scoured Germany's borders to find Slavs or other ethnic groups to ensure recruits had language skills. Hippel ran the show to begin with but then became commander of the Ist

Battalion. Promoted major in September 1940 he was involved in training for Operation 'Sealion', but during the preparations for 'Sealion' he had to quit the Brandenburgers in October 1940 after an incident related at length in Eric Lefevre's *Brandenburg Division* (see Bibliography page 94) that led to his court-martial. He and his men had been ordered to take an oath that they would undertake any mission proposed to them by the OKW. This went against the principle that the Brandenburgers' missions were voluntary and Hippel was not prepared to accept this. His argument was that it was dangerous enough to be sent into enemy territory — often in the enemy uniforms. Capture in almost every case would mean execution for spying. The only way to achieve this was by using volunteers who could refuse a mission if it seemed to be suicidal. He lost his job for refusing to administer the oath — which, interestingly, never was administered. He was replaced initially by Maj Kewisch, then von Aulock before Lt-Col Paul Haehling von Lanzenhauer became CO on 28 November 1940. Lt Wilhelm Walther took over command of Ist Battalion.

OTTO SKORZENY
(1908–1975)

Skorzeny was born in Vienna, Austria, to a father who was an engineer. While studying to follow in his father's footsteps at the Technical University in 1926–31 he gained the duelling scars that would later earn him the nickname 'Scarface', joined the right-wing Freikorps movement of mostly ex-soldiers and became a member of the Heimwehr local defence force. In 1930 he joined the emerging Nazi Party and immediately before the outbreak of World War II worked as a business manager for a building contractor. In 1939 he joined the IInd Reserve Battalion of the SS's Leibstandarte Adolf Hitler, the Führer's personal bodyguard, which was stationed in Berlin Lichterfelde. Skorzeny saw service during the invasion of France in 1940 and the attack on the Soviet Union in 1941, when he won the Iron Cross, Second Class. For much of 1942 he was stationed in Berlin as an engineering officer with a reserve regiment but in the autumn secured a post with 3rd SS Panzer Division Totenkopf. In April 1943 he transferred to Section VI of the *Reichssicherheitshauptamt*, the state security department of the SS. The section was headed by Walter Schellenberg and was responsible for political and, increasingly,

Above: Skorzeny in custody after his capture in Austria on 16 May 1945. He was a university student in Vienna and it was during these days that student duelling was prevalent. It was during the tenth of his fifteenth duels that the famous scar on his left cheek was incurred and would give rise to the nickname 'Scarface'. *US Army*

Above: SS Oberststurmbannführer Otto Skorzeny became Hitler's favourite commando after rescuing Mussolini.

military intelligence-gathering. The previous year it had established the Oranienberg special training course to raise the SS's equivalent of the Brandenburgers and Skorzeny was ordered to find and train recruits. These became known as the *Friedenthaler Jagdverbände* (Friedenthal Hunting Groups) after their base, a park and hunting lodge close to Berlin.

Skorzeny's rise to public fame opened with the rescue of Italian dictator Benito Mussolini in September 1943. He was specially selected to conduct the mission by Hitler and thereafter became one of his favourites. Skorzeny was permitted to expand his special forces and he gained some control of various specialist weapons, such as the Kriegsmarine's midget submarines, and the Luftwaffe's Kampfgruppe 200, which carried out special airborne missions. The Führer's faith in him was further confirmed during the 1944 bomb plot. On 20 July Skorzeny was on a Vienna-bound train stopped in the Berlin suburb of Lichterfelde when news of the coup attempt reached him. He immediately retraced his steps to the Bendlerstrasse, home of the Oberkommando der Wehrmacht, and set about aiding officers loyal to Hitler who crushed the plot. Skorzeny continued to carry out special operations until the end of the war, mostly memorably in Budapest during the following October and in the Ardennes in December. In the final months of the conflict he organised attacks by frogmen on Remagen bridge, conducting operations on the Eastern Front and attempted to organise Werewolf resistance bands in the so-called National Redoubt in the Bavaria Alps.

Skorzeny was arrested by US troops near Steiermark on 15 May and in September 1947 was tried for war crimes by a US military court at Dachau. The charges, relating to the murder of US prisoners at Malmédy in the Ardennes, were not proved and Skorzeny was acquitted. After working for the historical section of the US Army for a brief period he was rearrested by the postwar German authorities but escaped from a prison camp near Darmstadt in July 1949 and eventually fled to Spain where he enjoyed the protection of dictator Francisco Franco and adopted the cover name of Robert Steinbacher. Outwardly a business man in the import-export trade and real estate, it is believed that Skorzeny also founded a secret organisation known as *Die Spinne* (The Spider) that was supported by undiscovered funds from the Third Reich and aided around 500 former SS men in Germany to escape justice by mostly fleeing to South America.

ALEXANDER VON PFUHLSTEIN (1899–1976)

Born on 17 December 1899 in Danzig, Alexander von Pfuhlstein joined the German Army as a Fähnrich on 29 March 1917. He was promoted to lieutenant on 14 December 1917 and fought with 4th Grenadier Regiment. He rejoined the army when the Nazis came to power as a staff officer — the GSO Ia (operations) with 19th Infantry Division — in 3 November 1938 serving there until 10 January 1940 during which, on 1 June 1939, he was promoted lieutenant-colonel. The division took part in the Polish campaign fighting at first in the area around Zina Wolda where it took heavy casualties during the crossing of the river Warta and, later, the Vistula. Involved in the assault on Warsaw, after Poland surrendered the division was one of the units occupying the city until transferring to the west — the lower Rhine — in December. The 19th Division attacked across the Meuse in May 1940 but Pfuhlstein wasn't with them. He had transferred to become GSO Ia of 58th Infantry Division on 15 March 1940. This division,

COMMANDERS OF THE BRANDENBURG DIVISION, 1943–45

Brandenburg Division zbV 800

Maj-Gen Alexander von Pfuhlstein	1 April 1943–10 April 1944
Lt-Gen Fritz Kühlwein	10 April 1944–15 September 1944

Panzergrenadier Division Brandenburg

Lt-Gen Fritz Kühlwein	15 September 1944–16 October 1944
Maj-Gen Hermann Schulte-Heuthaus	16 October 1944–8 May 1945

FROM COMPANY TO DIVISION

**Bau-lehr-Kompanie zbV 800
'Deutsche Kompanie'**
Founded on 25 October 1939.

**Bau-Lehr-Bataillon zbV 800
'Brandenburg'**
On 15 December 1939, the company was enlarged to become a battalion of four companies, a motorcycle platoon, a paratroop platoon. Other specialised units were later attached (see page 15).

**Lehr-Regiment zbV 800
'Brandenburg'**
On 12 October 1940, the battalion was enlarged to become a regiment of three battalions with attached special companies (see page 40).

**Lehr-Division zbV 800
'Brandenburg'**
Between late 1942 and January 1943, the regiment was transformed into a division (see page 40), with specialised units such as von Koenen's Tropical Company.

**Panzergrenadier-Division
'Brandenburg'**
From 13 September 1943, the unit was no longer used for special operations and was organised along standard lines (see page 41).

Other Units
In summer 1942, the *Küstenjäger-Kompanie* was formed, the equivalent of the Special Boat Service.

Arabische Brigade
A volunteer force, fighting from 1940 onwards in Lebanon, Syria, Iraq and Iran, later with Kurdish allies in the Caucasus.

Deutsch-Arabische Legion
Mixed German-Arabian membership, operated mainly in Tunisia.

as part of XXIII Corps, advanced through Luxembourg and France to Verdun before moving south to Toul. It spent the rest of 1940 in Belgium designated part of the third wave of Operation 'Sealion' before the unit moved east, to Poland, in spring 1941. It would serve on the Eastern Front for the rest of the war, as part of Army Group North, attacking through Riga and Pleshkov in June 1941 and besieging Leningrad. Von Pfuhlstein became commander of the IInd Battalion of Infantry Regiment 18 on 1 March 1941 and then commanded Infantry Regiment 77 from 29 July 1941 to 2 March 1942, being promoted colonel on 1 February 1942. He became commander of Infantry Regiment 154 on 1 March 1942 serving with that unit until the autumn. It was as commander of IR154 that he won the Knight's Cross on 17 August 1942 in the Demjansk Pocket.

Pfuhlstein took over command of the newly created Brandenburg Division on 1 April 1943 and was involved in its change from a special operations unit to a much larger division — of 14,000 men. He was promoted major-general on 1 July 1943, but although during his time as commander the division took part in some notable actions — such as the occupation of Cos and Leros (see pages 36–7) — the writing was on the wall for the Brandenburgers, whose cause was not helped when Pfuhlstein was implicated in the anti-Nazi *Schwarze Kapelle* resistance movement. He was dismissed after just over a year in command on 10 April 1944 and discharged on 14 September 1944. He died on 20 December 1976 having lived postwar in Bad Homburg near Frankfurt am Main.

FRITZ KÜHLWEIN (1892–1976)

Pfuhlstein's position was taken by Lt-Gen Fritz Kühlwein, who assumed command of the division on 10 April 1944. Born on 29 November 1892 in Hatten/Weissenburg, Fritz Kühlwein entered the pre-World War I Reichsheer as a *Fahnenjunker* — a candidate for a regular commission — on 17 July 1912. He joined Infantry Regiment 97 as a lieutenant on 18 February 1914 and fought on the Eastern Front, particularly around Dünaburg (Daugavpils) in southeast Latvia, on the Western Dvina River. In December 1917 the regiment was transferred to the west to take part in Ludendorff's spring offensive, fighting around the Somme and Ancre. Part of the thrust that reached Noyon, the regiment would fight hard defensive battles as the Spring Offensive ground to a halt and the Allied armies started the offensive that would bring them victory. The regiment was disbanded on 19 September 1918.

Kühlwein's served in the Reichswehr — the standing army of the Weimar Republic and opening years of the Third Reich — being promoted lieutenant-colonel on 1 August

1936 and becoming commander of the IInd Battalion of Infantry Regiment 56 on 12 October 1937. As a major he wrote *Schützenzug im Gefecht* (The Infantry Platoon in Battle) published by Mittler & Son in 1936 and in 1938 as a lieutenant-colonel *Gefechtstaktik des verstärkten Bataillons* (Battle Tactics of the strengthened Battalion).

Promoted colonel on 1 April 1939, he took command of Infantry Ersatz (training) Regiment 73 in October 1939, before moving to command IR55 (home station Würzburg) on 15 January 1940. After taking part in the assault on the west, Kühlwein moved to command IR133 — part of 45th Infantry Division — on 15 October 1940, a position he held until 27 February 1942 when he took command of the division itself. The division had moved from the west to the Eastern Front in June 1941 and opened its campaign in Russia by attacking the fortress of Brest-Litovsk. Promoted major-general on 1 April 1942, he led the division for over a year, the latter part of which it spent in the area of Voronezh. Promoted lieutenant-general on 1 January 1943, he left 45th Infantry on 29 April 1943, and was subsequently chosen to command the Brandenburg Division, taking up the role on 13 April 1944. During his time as CO the division became a Panzergrenadier Division, fighting in Serbia as part of Army Group F, and he left shortly afterwards in October 1944 (just at about the time that part of the division became Festung Division Rhodos (Fortress Division Rhodes). On 29 December 1944 he took over command of Training and Replacement Division 401 located in Wehrkreis I, garrisoned on Königsberg in East Prussia. In March 1945 he took command of Feld Ersatz Division 149 based in the Netherlands, before surrendering in May. In later years he lived in Bielefeld and died in 1976.

Below: Hermann Schulte-Heuthaus

HERMANN SCHULTE-HEUTHAUS (1898–1979)

The last commander of the Brandenburgers was born on 15 January 1898 at Klein Weissensee in East Prussia. Hermann Schulte-Heuthaus joined the Reichsheer as an officer candidate on 14 October 1914, and went on to be commissioned into 4th Guards Regiment serving from 10 March 1915 as a lieutenant. He fought bravely during World War I, winning the Iron Cross, First and Second Classes. The regiment survived the war but was disbanded on 30 April 1920, Schulte-Heuthaus along with it, and he had to wait until 15 September 1934 before he could resume his military career, rejoining the Reichswehr as a captain. On 1 October 1937 he took over command of the 4th Company of the NCO school at Potsdam, moving on to run the Potsdam Infantry School from 1 September 1939. He was promoted lieutenant-colonel on 1 August 1940, and on 1 May 1941 he finally got the chance to lead a unit in the field when he took over *Krad-Schütz-Bataillon* (Motorcycle Infantry Battalion) Nr 25, which he led until 28 February 1942. After the battles of the winter he was awarded the Knight's Cross on 23 January 1942.

On 25 March 1942 Schulte-Heuthaus joined Erwin Rommel's Panzerarmee Afrika staff as IIa — adjutant. He was promoted colonel on 1 April 1942 and from then on played an important role as a staff officer — together with Lt-Col Siegfried Westphal, Schulte-Heuthaus was involved in planning the great offensive east that began on 25 May 1942 and would take Rommel's troops to El Alamein. Briefly taking over command of 90th Light Division between 17 and 22 September 1942 — he continued on Rommel's staff when, on 1 October 1942, Panzerarmee Afrika became the Deutsch-Italienische Panzerarmee (German-Italian

BRANDENBURGER HOLDERS OF THE KNIGHT'S CROSS WITH OAK LEAVES

Name	Rank	Unit	Date
Siegfried Grabert	Capt	Lehr Regiment Brandenburg zbV 800	6 November 1943
Karl-Heinz Oesterwitz	Lt-Col	Panzergrenadier Regiment Brandenburg	10 February 1945
Max Wandery	Maj	Panzergrenadier Regiment Brandenburg	16 March 1945

BRANDENBURGER HOLDERS OF THE KNIGHT'S CROSS

Name	Rank	Unit	Date
Erhard Afheldt	Lt	Panzergrenadier Division Brandenburg	17 March 1945
Wilhelm Bröckerhoff	Maj	Panzergrenadier Division Brandenburg	7 May 1945
Erich von Bruckner	Col	Panzergrenadier Division Brandenburg	8 April 1945
Adrian von Foelkersam	2-Lt	Lehr Regiment Brandenburg zbV 800	14 September 1942
Siegfried Grabert (1)	Lt	Lehr Regiment Brandenburg zbV 800	10 June 1941
Hans-Wolfram Knaak (2)	Capt	Lehr Regiment Brandenburg zbV 800	3 November 1942
Friedrich von Koenen (3)	Capt	Brandenburg Division zbV 800	16 September 1943
Erhard Lange (4)	Lt	Lehr Regiment Brandenburg zbV 800	15 January 1943
Werner Lau	2-Lt	Lehr Regiment Brandenburg zbV 800	9 December 1942
Helmut von Leipzig (5)	2-Lt	Panzergrenadier Division Brandenburg	28 April 1945
Karl-Heinz Oesterwitz	Lt	Lehr Regiment Brandenburg zbV 800	30 April 1943
Alexander von Pfuhlstein (6)	Maj-Gen	154th Infantry Division	1942
Ernst Prohaska (7)	2-Lt	Lehr Regiment Brandenburg zbV 800	16 September 1942
Erich Röseke (8)	Lt	Panzergrenadier Division Brandenburg	14 April 1945
Konrad Steidl (9)	Capt	Brandenburg Division zbV 800	26 January 1944
Wilhelm Walther	Lt	Bau Lehr battalion Brandenburg zbV 800	24 June 1940
Max Wandery	Lt	Brandenburg Division zbV 800	9 January 1944

(1) Grabert was an early recruit to the Brandenburgers but was killed in July 1942 leading the 2nd Battalion's 8th Company, which suffered 87 casualties, in a successful attack to take bridges over the Don River near Bataisk for the 13th Panzer Division during the drive into the Caucasus.

(2) Acting commander of the 2nd Battalion's 8th Company, he was killed in action while defending the recently captured Dünaberg bridges over the Dvina River in Latvia on 26 June 1941, during the first days of Operation 'Barbarossa'.

(3) Nicknamed 'Fritz', Koenen came from a farming family in southwest Africa and was commander of the regiment's Tropical Company (later battalion) that served in North Africa from 1941.

(4) Gained the award for his leadership in Operation 'Shamil', a behind-the-lines mission to supply Muslims in the Caucasus with the arms and ammunition needed to revolt against the Soviet Union in 1942. 'Shamil' failed and only Lange and one other man, a Tartar, made it safely back to German lines.

(5) Commanded the Brandenburger detachment participating in Operation 'Dora', a reconnaissance into Niger and Chad to assess the feasibility of severing alleged Anglo-French supply routes in the area of Lake Chad in mid-1942.

(6) Pfuhlstein was removed from command of the Brandenburg Division in April 1944 for involvement in anti-Hitler conspiracies. He won his Knight's Cross in the Demjansk Pocket during 1942 while commander of a regular army unit.

(7) A Russian-speaking ethnic German who grew up along the Volga River, Prohaska led a platoon from the 2nd Battalion's 8th Company that captured a bridge over the Bjelaja River during the push on Maikop in the northern Caucasus during August 1942. The operation was successful but he was killed.

(8) Received for leading a group of men from the 6th Company of the 1st Regiment's 2nd Battalion to safety after spending 11 days behind Red Army lines in Poland, despite being wounded on several occasions.

(9) Received the award for commanding the division's 1st Battalion, 2nd Regiment, during successful operations against Tito's partisans in Bosnia.

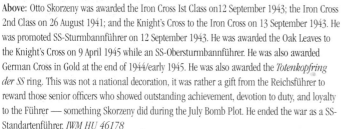

Above: Otto Skorzeny was awarded the Iron Cross Ist Class on12 September 1943; the Iron Cross 2nd Class on 26 August 1941; and the Knight's Cross to the Iron Cross on 13 September 1943. He was promoted SS-Sturmbannführer on 12 September 1943. He was awarded the Oak Leaves to the Knight's Cross on 9 April 1945 while an SS-Obersturmbannführer. He was also awarded German Cross in Gold at the end of 1944/early 1945. He was also awarded the *Totenkopfring der SS* ring. This was not a national decoration, it was rather a gift from the Reichsführer to reward those senior officers who showed outstanding achievement, devotion to duty, and loyalty to the Führer — something Skorzeny did during the July Bomb Plot. He ended the war as a SS-Standartenführer. *IWM HU 46178*

Above right: Lt-Col Wilhelm Walther won his Knight's cross on 24 June 1940 while leading the assault troops of the 4th Company of the Brandenburg Battalion. The story is recounted on pages 17–8. *Bundesarchiv*

Right: Siegfried Grabert was born on 11 January 1916 in Schorndorf an der Rems, Kreis Waiblingen, Württemberg. He was awarded the Iron Cross Ist Class on 2 June 1940; the Iron Cross 2nd Class on 12 May 1940; and the Knight's Cross to the Iron Cross on 10 June 1941 as a lieutenant in the 8th Company of Lehr Regiment Brandenburg then attached to XVIII Army Corps, Twelfth Army. He died on 25 July 1942 in area of Rostov, on the Eastern Front as a captain while commanding the 8th Company of the regiment. He was awarded the Oak Leaves to the Knight's Cross posthumously on 6 November 1943. He was also holder of the Infantry Assault Badge in silver. *Bundesarchiv*

Panzer Army), retreating back to Tunisia after Montgomery's victory at El Alamein. He escaped capture when German forces surrendered in Tunisia in early May 1943 and became commander of Panzerfüsilier Regiment Grossdeutschland on 7 July 1943 at a time when Grossdeutschland was involved in the battle of Kursk. (In October 1942, at the same time as similar renamings throughout the German Army, Infantry Regiment Grossdeutschland Nr 1 was retitled 'Grenadier Regiment Grossdeutschland' and Infantry Regiment GD 2 was renamed 'Füsilier Regiment Grossdeutschland.' This was done in homage to the units in the army of Frederick the Great, whom Hitler greatly admired. *Schützen* [infantry] regiments in Panzer divisions were at the same time renamed Panzergrenadier regiments. Rank titles for infantrymen were also renamed, *Schütze* [Private] becoming *Grenadier* or *Panzergrenadier*. For the Füsilier Regiment of Grossdeutschland, *Füsilier* also became the rank title for a private serving in the unit.)

Schulte-Heuthaus held the position in Füsilier Regiment Grossdeutschland for about two months — until 4 September 1943 — when he was wounded in action. After six months of recuperation, he then commanded the Ersatz (Reserve) Brigade in Cottbus from 27 March to 15 October 1944, before assuming command of the Panzergrenadier Division Brandenburg which he led until the end of the war. Brandenburg fought mainly on the Eastern Front, in the latter stages as part of the Grossdeutschland Panzer Corps which was finally destroyed by Soviet forces in Czechoslovakia in 1945.

After the war Schulte-Heuthaus returned to Berlin, living there until his death on 28 December 1979.

FRIEDRICH 'FRITZ' VON KOENEN (1916–44)

Born on 28 June 1916 in Danzig-Langfuhr, Friedrich von Koenan was the son of a South African farmer and was in South Africa when World War II started. He (and some 450 others) rushed back to Germany to join up. Many of these men — including Koenen — ended up in the Brandenburgers, 'Fritz' being promoted Oberleutnant and made commander of 13th Company — the regiment's training unit. On 28 October 1941 von Koenen and some 300 hand-picked men — the *Tropen-Kompanie* (Tropical Company) Brandenburg — left Germany for Africa. Rommel was not in favour of clandestine operations at first, and was not keen on the Brandenburgers' raison d'être — action behind the enemy's lines. However, as soon as the British Long Range Desert Group started operating, Rommel changed his view and it wasn't long before von Koenen's men had won Rommel over.

They proved to be excellent commandos and the desert proved an excellent battleground for such troops. Roger Bender and Richard Law's splendid book on the Afrika Korps (see Bibliography page 93) identifies a number of these desert missions by the Brandenburgers, designated *Abteilung* von Koenen in early 1943, including the one on which Capt von Koenen won his Knight's Cross. It took place on 26 December 1942 when he led a glider-borne unit that destroyed a railway bridge at Sidi bou Bakr. He was awarded the Knight's Cross on 16 September 1943.

Recalled from the desert he commanded the IIIrd Battalion of the 4th Regiment of the Brandenburgers in Greece and Yugoslavia, where he met his death. On 20 August 1944, as an lieutenant-colonel, he was ambushed by partisans in Visegrad, Herzegovina. Koenen, his driver and adjutant were all mortally wounded and the partisans looted his Knight's Cross as he lay dying.

The German Soldier's Ten Commandments
[in every German Soldier's Paybook]

1. While fighting for victory the German soldier will observe the rules of chivalrous warfare. Cruelties and senseless destruction are below his standard.

2. Combatants will be in uniform or will wear specially introduced and clearly distinguishable badges. Fighting in plain clothes or without such badges is prohibited.

3. No enemy who has surrendered will be killed, including partisans and spies. They will be duly punished by courts.

4. P.O.W. will not be ill-treated or insulted. While arms, maps, and records are to be taken away from them, their personal belongings will not be touched.

5. Dum-dum bullets are prohibited; also no other bullets may be transformed into dum-dum.

6. Red Cross Institutions are sacrosanct. Injured enemies are to be treated in a humane way. Medical personnel and army chaplains may not be hindered in the execution of their medical, or clerical activities.

7. The civilian population is sacrosanct. No looting nor wanton destruction is permitted to the soldier. Landmarks of historical value or buildings serving religious purposes, art, science, or charity are to be especially respected. Deliveries in kind made, as well as services rendered by the population, may only be claimed if ordered by superiors and only against compensation.

8. Neutral territory will never be entered nor passed over by planes, nor shot at; it will not be the object of warlike activities of any kind.

9. If a German soldier is made a prisoner of war he will tell his name and rank if he is asked for it. Under no circumstances will he reveal to which unit he belongs, nor will he give any information about German military, political, and economic conditions. Neither promises nor threats may induce him to do so.

10. Offenses against the a/m matters of duty will be punished. Enemy offences against the principles under 1 to 8 are to be reported. Reprisals are only permissible on order of higher commands.

ASSESSMENT

Below: Oberleutnant Siegfried Grabert. The most famous and engaging officer in the Brandenburg Regiment. In May 1940 he was the leader of a platoon of the 4th Company with the task of taking the bridges over the Juliana Canal intact and preventing the destruction of the locks at Nieuport. He was one of two Brandenburgers who removed the explosive charges from the Nieuport bridge. He then commanded the 8th Company and during the Yugoslavian campaign, seized the bridges over the Vardar on 6 April 1941. This success brought about the award of the Knight's Cross of the Iron Cross the following 10 June, the second in the regiment. Grabert fell the following year at the head of his company in Russia. *TRH Pictures*

The Brandenburgers conducted special operations from the invasion of Poland in 1939 until around mid-1943, when they increasingly took on more conventional roles and were effectively replaced by the SS's own special forces under Otto Skorzeny. Assessing the qualities and effectiveness of the Brandenburgers is fraught with difficulties not least because the unit's reports and combat diaries were mostly destroyed during the war. What evidence remains is fragmentary, anecdotal and often downright contradictory. Some of the claims made for the unit undoubtedly need to be treated with a good measure of scepticism, yet there is sufficient hard evidence to suggest that the Brandenburgers did make a significant contribution to the Nazi war effort, one out of all proportion to the size of the unit, particularly in the years of success between 1939 and 1942. In these years the Brandenburgers effectively spearheaded Germany's Blitzkrieg attacks, seizing key objectives such as intact bridges that allowed the momentum of the armoured thrusts to be maintained — a central plank of such offensives. That they did so often wearing the uniforms of the enemy or civilian clothes is a controversial topic and a matter of debate in respect of internationally accepted military law.

These tactical victories at the forefront of the Blitzkrieg were also matched by strategic triumphs, especially with regard to their missions in 1941 to keep the Danube River open and protect the Romanian oil fields that fuelled German's war effort. However, the enlargement of the unit, from battalion to regiment and then to division, was paralleled by a change in its character. Original recruits were chosen for qualities other than their knowledge of military skills, not least their expertise in foreign languages and customs. It was relatively straightforward to fill a battalion or regiment with such men and give them military training, but surely not a division. Equally important is the fact that Germany's Blitzkrieg attacks ended in late 1942 and with them went the need for a spearhead force like the Brandenburgers. The swift descent on Leros in late 1943 can be seen as their last classic operation. More and more from the latter part of 1942 the Brandenburgers began to undertake conventional operations and campaigned in large-scale sweeps against partisans. Neither were suitable employment for such a specialist force and it appears that, as losses mounted, morale deteriorated. Indeed, many of the first recruits, by this stage middle-ranking officers, chose to seek employment elsewhere, not least with the Waffen-SS and the SS's own special forces.

Ultimately the Brandenburgers fell victim to Nazi power politics, chiefly the struggle between the SS and the *Abwehr* that gathered pace in late autumn 1942. It is clear that the *Abwehr*'s senior figures, not least Canaris and Oster, were involved in anti-Nazi plots and their fate — and that of the organisation as a whole — was sealed when the much more ruthless intelligence and security services of the SS gathered firm evidence against them during 1943. As an integral part of the *Abwehr* the Brandenburgers were branded guilty by association and, although there appears to be little hard evidence that any were involved in the anti-Nazi resistance, the unit probably became seen by the Nazi hierarchy as politically unreliable. Consequently, if Hitler was to have special forces in the latter part of the war they had to be sourced elsewhere and preferably from among the ranks of clearly committed Nazis whose loyalty was unimpeachable. Otto Skorzeny, who had joined the Nazi Party in 1930 and the Waffen-SS in 1939, was the ideal candidate to lead such units as was amply demonstrated by his role in defeating the anti-Hitler plotters in Berlin during late July 1944.

Skorzeny's rise to prominence as head of Nazi special forces came at a time when the Third Reich's fortunes were declining fast. The string of sweeping victories of the first half of the war had given way to defeat after defeat between 1943 and 1945, a catalogue of disasters only infrequently punctuated by small-scale and temporary victories. Thus while the Brandenburgers fought to expand the Third Reich, Skorzeny's troops struggled to prevent its inevitable collapse. A second difference between the two forces was that the Brandenburgers received scant publicity for their exploits, possibly because of the significantly non-Aryan nature of the unit and certainly because the wider armed forces were also covering themselves in glory during their heyday. In contrast Skorzeny became a very well-known Nazi hero and recipient of many awards at a time when the regular German armed forces could provide little good news. His missions were used as a not insignificant propaganda weapon to boost the

Above: Skorzeny's rescue of Mussolini did much to foster the commando's image. Postwar, as a brilliant self-publicist, his writings did the same.
Bundesarchiv

sagging morale of the German people at a time when bad news from the front was an almost daily event. The legend of Skorzeny grew after World War II, not least because the man himself was a great self-publicist and often made somewhat exaggerated claims. It is undoubtedly true that his rescue of Mussolini in 1943 and the Budapest mission the following year were brilliant coups, planned and carried out swiftly and surgically with little loss of life. They might also be regarded as much political as military operations that had not inconsiderable and wider implications — Mussolini was kept out of Allied hands and Hungary stayed within the Axis orbit — but they could not prevent Italy surrendering or Hungary being overrun by the Red Army. Skorzeny's role in the Ardennes offensive in late 1944 was ambitiously planned but little thought was given to the practicalities of raising and training such a specialist unit as the 150th Panzer Brigade. This was Hitler's fault and not Skorzeny's. In the event the brigade reverted to a conventional role within the first few days of Operation '*Wacht am Rhein*' and the teams of the English-speaking Stielau detachment had scant success, apart from making the Allies extremely jittery for a short time. Skorzeny was christened 'the most dangerous man in Europe' by his foes due to his early successes, but even the most dangerous man in Europe could not stave off Nazi Germany's ultimate defeat with a few thousand special forces, no matter how audacious his operations.

REFERENCE

THE BRANDENBURG COMMANDOS

Elite Forces of the Third Reich

Elite Units of the German Armed Forces
1933 - 1945

THIRD REICH FACTBOOK

This is an apolitical site dedicated to

Comparatively little has been written about the Brandenburgers and the *Abwehr*, while Skorzeny's exploits, particularly Operation '*Greif*', have received somewhat greater coverage. However, a note of caution needs to be sounded, not least because of the convoluted histories of these special forces, which went through several transformations during the war. It is particularly true of the Brandenburgers that the scarce material available is often contradictory and confusing. Different references provide different information, disagree over the details of their operations, and even spell names differently and provide various dates for events that are known about. There is even some doubt that missions mentioned by some authors ever actually took place. The picture for Skorzeny's operations is somewhat clearer, most are recorded with a higher degree of accuracy, but Skorzeny, who produced several books on his wartime career, was prone to embellishing the facts, while skirting around the despicable aspects of Nazism. As a general rule the internet sites are interesting but often retread the same information but in truncated form. Many are little more than basic and some badly written, although a number do have interesting and unusual pictures depicting members and operations of these rarely photographed units.

WEBSITES

http://www.panzerworld.net/Pzdivs/PZB150.htm
A resume of the role of the 150th Panzer Brigade during Operation '*Wacht am Rhein*'. It comprises a short section on the unit's creation and performance and is linked to a useful order of battle.

http://www.joric.com/conspiracy/Oster.htm
This details the various anti-Nazi conspiracies instigated by or involving Hans Oster, Canaris's deputy in the *Abwehr*, that were to lead to both their downfalls and impact on the Brandenburgers. The site also includes pages on specific conspiracies, such as 'U-7', that directly implicated the *Abwehr* in treasonable acts.

http://www.skalman.nu/third-reich/heer-panzergr-div-brandenburg.htm
A useful order of battle for the Panzergrenadier Division *Brandenburg* that also includes brief details of its commanders and areas of operation. The same site has a similar list for the *Brandenburg* division.

http://www.forces70.freeserve.co.uk/Brandenberg/commanders.htm.
A site that runs through much the same information as the previous entry but in greater

detail. It also provides information on the Brandenburger regiment and in most cases names battalion and company commanders. The same site also includes pages on various Brandenburg missions, including Maikop and north Africa, as well as information on recruitment and training and holders of the Knight's Cross.

http://www.eliteforces.freewire.co.uk/Brandenburg/afghan.htm
This provides details of one of the Brandenburgers' least covered missions, that in Afghanistan during 1941. It is part of a much more extensive site that also provides information on Operations 'Sealion' and 'Felix', Bucharest in 1944 and Romania during 1941. Additional pages given brief information on uniforms and insignia. The same site provides similar coverage of the 500th SS Parachute Battalion that was part of Skorzeny's command during the war.

http:home.wxs.n1~graspol/frame 25 01.htm
A very basic and episodic account of the career of the Brandenburgers that also has brief passages on the *Abwehr* during the interwar years.

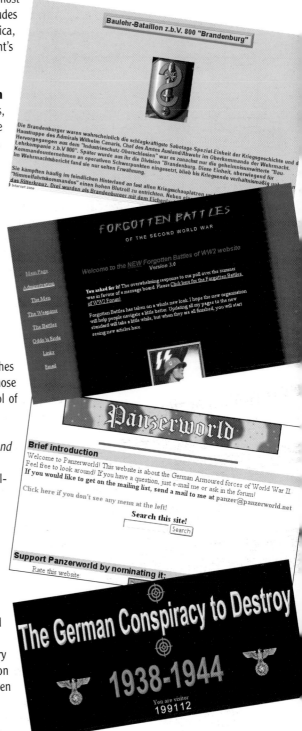

BIBLIOGRAPHY

Ailsby, Christopher: *SS: Roll of Infamy*; Brown Books, 1997.
An encyclopaedia of a bibliography of leading figures in the various branches of the SS. Among the hundreds of personalities covered are entries on those involved in the political struggle between the SS and *Abwehr* for control of Nazi intelligence-gathering operations.

Bender, Roger James, and Law, Richard D.: *Uniforms, Organisation and History of the Afrikakorps*, R. James Bender Publishing, 1973.
A terrific source book of information on Rommel's desert armies, well-illustrated, original and a mine of information.

Berthold, Will: *Brandenburg Division*; Mayflower Books Ltd, 1973.
Although of dubious accuracy and best treated as a work of fiction, Berthold recounts Brandenburg activities during the war, concentrating on the Eastern Front and the Balkans. It is a lively read and does include brief passages that seem to tally with known events and personalities.

Cooper, Matthew, and Lucas, James: *Panzer Grenadiers*; Macdonald and Jane's, 1977.
A general overview of the development of Germany's motorised infantry units that also includes a study of the Panzergrenadier Division Brandenburg's bitter struggle to hold the line of the Neisse River between Muskau and Görlitz in April 1945.

Foley, Charles: *Commando Extraordinary*, Arms and Armour Press, 1987.
First published in the 1950s it was written with help by the so-called 'most dangerous man in Europe' and remains one of the best — if exaggerated — accounts of the life and times of Skorzeny during World War II. It includes a section on the subject's trial at Nuremberg.

Höhne, H: *Canaris*; Bertelsmann, 1976.
A standard text on the head of the *Abwehr* that charts his rise and the fall of Germany's intelligence-gathering service

Kessler, Leo: *Kommando*; Leo Cooper, 1995.
Writing under his frequently used pseudonym, Charles Whiting recounts in lively style operations conducted by the Brandenburgers and Otto Skorzeny as well as the futile resistance efforts of the teenage Werewolves at the end of the war and the Nazi attempts to establish a National Redoubt in Bavaria at the end of the war. However, it suffers from poor editing and details of some events do not match those found in other sources.

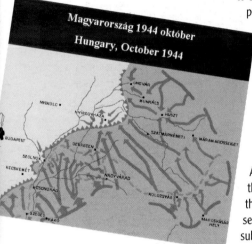

Kurowski, Franz: *The Brandenburgers — Global Mission*; J. J. Fedorowicz, 1997.
A wide-ranging volume that recounts the history of the Brandenburgers and includes some interesting sections on the Brandenburgers most distant missions, including operations in Afghanistan Burma, India, Iran and Iraq that receive virtually no coverage elsewhere.

Lefevre, Eric (trans. Finel, Julia): *Brandenburg Division: Commandos of the Reich*; Histoire & Collections, 1999.
An excellent and detailed account of the Brandenburgers from their earliest days to their last battles as a panzergrenadier division. It also contains copious appendices that give details of the unit's changing organisation and commanders and there is a selection of rare photographs of operations and personalities. Of all the books on the subject, this appears the most measured and accurate.

Lucas, James: *Kommando — German Special Forces of World War II*; Arms and Armour Press, 1985.
A wide-ranging look at Nazi Germany's special forces on land, at sea and in the air. The greater part of the book concentrates on various land forces, particularly the major operations conducted by the Brandenburgers, specialist Luftwaffe paratrooper units and Otto Skorzeny. It also details the rivalry between the SD and *Abwehr*.

Lucas, James: *Storm Eagles — German Airborne Forces in World War II*; Arms and Armour Press, 1988.
Although it concentrates mainly on the Luftwaffe's parachute arm, this highly illustrated volume has chapters on the rescue of Mussolini in September 1943, the battle for Leros the following November and the Ardennes offensive in late 1944 that include reference to both the Brandenburgers and Otto Skorzeny. There is also a chapter that deals entirely with the 500th SS Parachute Battalion's attempt to kill or capture Tito in May 1944.

Lucas, James: *The Last Year of the Germany Army, May 1944–May 1945*; Arms and Armour Press, 1994.
Although wide-ranging in scope, it does include passages that look at the complex and confusing array of units that served under Otto Skorzeny and also gives a brief summary of Operation 'Panzerfaust', his coup in Budapest in October 1944.

Lumsden, Robin: *A Collector's Guide to Third Reich Militaria*; Ian Allan Publishing Ltd, 2000.
Essential handy reference.

Pallud, Jean-Paul: *Ardennes, 1944: Peiper & Skorzeny*; Osprey Publishing Ltd, 1987.
One of the ever-popular Osprey series that recounts the story of two specialist units

during the Battle of the Bulge in late 1944, including Operation 'Greif' conducted by Skorzeny's 150th Panzer Brigade.

Parssinen, Terry M: *The Oster Conspiracy of 1938 — The Unknown Story of the Military Plot to Kill Hitler and Avert World War II*; HarperCollins, 2003.
An indepth look at the failed attempt by a circle of German officers, diplomats and others to halt the slide to war by assassination on the eve of the conflict. It includes details of the *Abwehr*'s involvement in the plot including the activities of Canaris's deputy, Hans Oster.

Ramsey, Winston (ed), et al: *After the Battle*, Battle of Britain Prints International.
This remarkable magazine and range of books provides a plethora of Brandenburg-related material, including: 'Gibraltar' in issue 21; 'Rescue of Mussolini' in issue 22; 'Operation Panzerfaust' in issue 40; 'The Battle for Leros' in issue 90; *Blitzkrieg in the West Then and Now* and *Battle of the Bulge Then and Now* (both by Jean-Paul Pallud). The level of research and meticulous detail make these publications hugely helpful.

Skorzeny, Otto (trans. David Johnston): M*y Commando Operations: The Memoirs of Hitler's Most Daring Commando*; Schiffer Publishing Limited, 1995.
Skorzeny tells his story in his own words and also recounts related matters such as the flight of Rudolph Hess, his assessment of German and Soviet military intelligence, and the massacre of US troops at Malmédy, Belgium, in late 1944.

Spaeter, Helmut: *The History of the Panzerkorps Grossdeutschland* (Vol. 3).
The final volume in the comprehensive account of undoubtedly the best of the non-Waffen-SS units in Nazi Germany's order of battle charts the history of the unit's latter battles as well as providing a history of the Brandenburgers as a commando unit, their development into the Panzergrenadier Division Brandenburg and the division's battles.

Schenk, Peter: *Invasion of England 1940: The Planning of Operation Sealion*; Conway Maritime Press Ltd, 1990
A detailed and extensive examination of the planning for the invasion of Britain.

Steffens, Hans von: *Salaam — Secret Commando to the Nile*; K. Vowinckel Verlag, 1960.
The memoirs of the *Abwehr* officer who planned the operation to infiltrate agents into Egypt during 1942.

Whiting, Charles: *Skorzeny*; Ballantine, 1972.
An highly illustrated account of the wartime career of the SS's most daring commander of special forces with details on his numerous operations.

Whiting, Charles: *Canaris*; New York, 1973.
An account of the career of Admiral Wilhelm Canaris, head of the *Abwehr*, Nazi Germany's intelligence service, from 19 January 1935 to February 1944 and who was subsequently executed for anti-Hitler activities.

Whiting, Charles: *Ardennes — The Secret War*; Century 1984.
The story behind the various clandestine operations planned and carried out during the Battle of the Bulge during late 1944.

INDEX